Cortical functions

D0224497

The human brain is the most complicated, wonderful and mysterious structure in the natural world. It is responsible for perception and movement; it allows us to think, learn, fear and dream. John Stirling's introductory text concentrates on the cerebral cortex, its structure, connections, functions and dysfunctions. Clinical descriptions and case studies support discussion of various forms of agnosia, aphasia and the split brain syndrome. Methods in neuropsychology are reviewed and comprehensive coverage given to the role of the brain in language, sensation, perception and movement.

John Stirling is Senior Lecturer in Psychology at Manchester Metropolitan University.

Routledge Modular Psychology

Series editors: Cara Flanagan is the Assessor for the Associated Examining Board (AEB) and an experienced A-level author. Kevin Silber is Senior Lecturer in Psychology at Staffordshire University. Both are A-level examiners in the UK.

The *Routledge Modular Psychology* series is a completely new approach to introductory level psychology, tailor-made to the new modular style of teaching. Each short book covers a topic in more detail than any large textbook can, allowing teacher and student to select material exactly to suit any particular course or project.

The books have been written especially for those students new to higher-level study, whether at school, college or university. They include specially designed features to help with technique, such as a model essay at an average level with an examiner's comments to show how extra marks can be gained. The authors are all examiners and teachers at the introductory level.

The *Routledge Modular Psychology* texts are all user-friendly and accessible and include the following features:

- practice essays with specialist commentary to show how to achieve a higher grade
- chapter summaries to assist with revision
- progress and review exercises
- glossary of key terms
- summaries of key research
- further reading to stimulate ongoing study and research
- website addresses for additional information
- cross-referencing to other books in the series

Also available in this series (titles listed by syllabus section):

ATYPICAL DEVELOPMENT AND ABNORMAL BEHAVIOUR

Psychopathology
John D. Stirling and Jonathan S. E. Hellewell

Therapeutic Approaches in Psychology
Susan Cave

BIO-PSYCHOLOGY

Awareness: Biorhythms, sleep and dreaming
Evie Bentley

The Physiological Basis of Behaviour: Neural and hormonal processes
Kevin Silber

COGNITIVE PSYCHOLOGY

Memory and Forgetting
John Henderson

Perception: Theory, development and organisation
Paul Rookes and Jane Willson (forthcoming)

COMPARATIVE PSYCHOLOGY

Evolutionary Explanations of Human Behaviour
John Gammon (forthcoming)

DEVELOPMENTAL PSYCHOLOGY

Early Socialisation: Sociability and attachment
Cara Flanagan

PERSPECTIVES AND RESEARCH

Controversies in Psychology
Philip Banyard

Ethical Issues in Psychology
Mike Cardwell (forthcoming)

Introducing Research and Data in Psychology: A guide to methods and analysis
Ann Searle

SOCIAL PSYCHOLOGY

Social Influences
Kevin Wren

Interpersonal Relationships
Diana Dwyer (forthcoming)

STUDY GUIDE

Exam Success in AEB Psychology
Paul Humphreys

OTHER TITLES

Health Psychology
Anthony Curtis (forthcoming)

Sport Psychology
Matt Jarvis

Cortical functions

John Stirling

London and New York

First published 2000
by Routledge
11 New Fetter Lane, London EC4P 4EE

Simultaneously published in the USA and Canada
by Routledge
29 West 35th Street, New York, NY 10001

Routledge is an imprint of the Taylor & Francis Group

© 2000 John Stirling

Typeset in Times and Frutiger by Taylor & Francis Books Ltd
Printed and bound in Great Britain by St Edmundsbury Press,
Bury St Edmunds, Suffolk

British Library Cataloguing in Publication Data
A catalogue record for this book is available from the British Library

Library of Congress Cataloging in Publication Data
Stirling, John, 1951–
Cortical Functions
p. cm. – (Routledge modular psychology)
Includes bibliographical references and index.
1. Cerebral cortex. 2. Neuropsychology. 3. Neuropsychiatry.
I. Series.
QP383.S84 1999
612.8'25–DC21   99–31483

ISBN 0–415–19266–8 (hbk)
ISBN 0–415–19267–6 (pbk)

To **Fred Finch** for awakening my interest in science, and **Reg Hayes** for instilling in me a sense of wonder about the brain.

Contents

Illustrations

Figures

Acknowledgements

The series editors and Routledge acknowledge the expert help of Paul Humphreys, Examiner and Reviser for A-level Psychology, in compiling the Study Aids section of each book in the series.

They also acknowledge the Associated Examining Board (AEB) for granting permission to use their examination material. The AEB do not accept responsibility for the answers or examiner comment in the Study Aids section of this book or any other book in the series.

The author and publishers would like to thank all the copyright holders of material reproduced in this volume for granting permission to include it. Every effort has been made to contact authors and copyright holders, but if proper acknowledgement has not been made, the copyright holder should contact the publishers.

1

The brain and psychological functioning

Introduction

The adult human brain is the most complicated, wonderful and mysterious structure in the natural world. To the naked eye, its outer surface looks bumpy and creased. Inside, it seems solid, with the consistency of stiff jelly, yet towards the centre, there are four quite large fluid filled cavities. Throughout life (even during deepest sleep) the brain remains active. In relation to the rest of the body, it uses disproportionately large amounts of fuel (glucose). To obtain this fuel, which arrives via the blood supply, it receives about 20% of the entire output of the heart. The brain is responsible for perception and movement. It allows us to think, learn, fear and dream. It weighs just 1200 grams.

In this chapter, I provide a 'potted' history of the beginnings of scientific research into the brain, and introduce you to some of the theories (and debates) that have surfaced as our understanding of this incredible biological machine has developed. The background I provide will help you to understand the context in which psychologists and other scientists have set about doing brain research.

Some history

Historical records from the Middle East suggest that the importance of the brain as a control centre was first considered at least 5000 years ago, although for many the heart was viewed as the organ of thinking and other mental processes. The ancient Greeks also debated the relative merits of heart and brain. Hippocrates and Plato both had some understanding of brain structure, and attributed various aspects of behaviour to it. Hippocrates warned against probing a wound in the brain in case it might lead to paralysis in the opposite side of the body. In Rome, the physician Galen, who spent a number of years working as a surgeon to gladiators, was also only too well aware of the effects that brain damage could have on behaviour.

However, the knowledge and understanding of these early writers was lost or forgotten for the next 1500 years or so of European history. Those with any interest in the brain concentrated on misguided attempts to find the location of the soul. Their search focused on easily identifiable brain structures including the pineal gland and the corpus callosum. Today, these same structures are known to be involved in the control of bodily rhythms and communication between the two sides of the brain respectively.

The localisation of function debate

The early researchers were also interested in the concept of *localisation of function*, although they concentrated their search within the fluid cavities (known as **ventricles**) mentioned earlier rather than the surrounding brain tissue. The basic idea of localisation of function is that different regions of the brain are involved in specific and separate aspects of psychological functioning. This idea certainly interested both Gall and his student Spurzheim, whose work represents the starting point of what we might call the modern era of brain–behaviour research. Gall (1785–1828) readily accepted that the brain, rather than the heart, was the control centre for mental function, and with

Spurzheim, the two made many important discoveries about the anatomy of the brain and spinal cord.

The rise and fall of phrenology

Gall thought that the brain consisted of 27 compartments or regional faculties. These ranged from common-sense ones such as language and perception to ambiguous and obscure ones including hope and self-esteem. According to Gall, the more a person used his or her faculties, the bigger the brain in that region grew, causing the shape of the skull to be distorted. Thus was born the 'science' of phrenology, which claimed to be able to describe an individual's personality and other 'faculties' on the basis of the physical size and shape of the skull.

Interest in phrenology gradually spread, receiving royal support when Queen Victoria had her children's heads measured and analysed. Gall and Spurzheim collected thousands of measurements, including a series taken from the skulls of 25 murderers, and even from an amorous widow who was described as having prominent features (bumps) behind her ears! Each observation simply confirmed the general theory, except that the number of faculties crept up to 35!

Doubts about phrenology first arose when it became apparent that the shape of the skull bore little relationship to the shape of the underlying brain. Obviously at the time, Gall and Spurzheim had no way of measuring the internal brain structure of living people, save for those rare instances of individuals surviving (and often not for very long) **open head injuries**. Actually, records show that Gall had access to a small number of such cases, and he is credited with providing the first full account of brain damage linked to loss of language (**aphasia**). Unfortunately, he seemed to regard these cases as being of only anecdotal interest, preferring instead to accumulate more and more measurements from members of the general population which 'confirmed' his ideas.

The French scientist Pierre Flourens provided the evidence which led people to begin to question the value of phrenology. Working with animals, he developed the technique of surgically removing small areas of brain tissue, and, after a period of recovery, observing the effects of the surgery on behaviour. (We now refer to these procedures as **lesion** and **ablation**, and they are described more extensively in Chapter 3). Using these techniques he was able to show that the brain region that Gall had thought responsible for the amorous behaviour of his famous widow actually appeared to co-ordinate balance!

Flourens' research led him to argue that the degree of behavioural impairment was as much linked to the *amount* of damage as to its *location*. This view undermines the principle of localisation of function that Gall and Spurzheim had promoted. Flourens also believed that undamaged regions could take over the responsibilities of damaged ones. This idea gave rise to the popular (but mistaken) belief that people only use a small proportion their brains, keeping other areas in reserve for learning new skills or replacing damaged areas.

Interest in aphasia

Despite Flourens' lack of enthusiasm for localisation of function, interest in it grew with the publication of a series of case-studies of aphasia. French researchers Bouillaud and Dax independently described patients they had seen who had lost the use of language after brain damage to the left side. These patients often became paralysed in the right side of their bodies too, despite no apparent loss in intelligence.

In 1861, Paul Broca described the case of 'Tan', so-called because this had become the only sound he could utter. However, he could understand speech well and could, for example, follow complicated instructions. In fact, in most other respects, he seemed normal, except that he too was paralysed on his right side. Broca proposed that Tan had suffered damage to the same area of brain (the left-frontal region, meaning on the left side towards the front) earlier identified as crucial for language production by Gall. When Tan died from an unrelated disease later that year, Broca conducted a post-mortem on his brain, and confirmed that he had indeed incurred left-frontal brain damage from a **stroke**.

Within two years, Broca had collected post-mortem data on eight similar cases. This research led him to conclude that language production depends on intact left-frontal function, and that, in more general terms, the two sides of the brain seem to control the opposite sides of the body. (In fact, neither of these ideas was new. The relationship of one side of the brain to the opposite side of the body had been described by Galen almost 2000 years earlier, and the link between left-sided damage and aphasia had first been proposed by Dax and Bouillaud in the 1830s.) Nevertheless, Broca seemed to gain the credit, and the region of brain (part of the left frontal **cortex**) he described is now known as Broca's area.

Soon, other regions of cortex were identified as being important for other aspects of language. In 1874, Carl Wernicke described two additional forms of aphasia, distinct from Broca's type. In **fluent aphasia**, the patient can speak at a normal rate, but what is said usually makes little sense. In **conduction aphasia**, the patient seems to understand what is said to them but is unaware of what they themselves are saying! Fluent aphasia occurred in individuals with damage to a region of their left temporal lobe (the brain area roughly behind and above the ear). In conduction aphasia there was evidence of damage to the connections between this region (now known as Wernicke's area) and Broca's area. Thus, within a few years, three different brain regions, all on the left side, had been identified as crucial for normal language. In 1892, Dejerine identified the cortical area (these days called the angular gyrus) related to the loss of the ability to read (known as **alexia**), and the localisation of function concept gained considerably in credibility.

Match up the names with the 'ideas', and write one sentence describing the idea itself:

Flourens	anti-localisation
Gall	left-brain language
Galen	27 faculties
Dax	brain damage and loss of function

Progress exercise

Mass action and equipotentiality

Despite the evidence presented in the previous section, it would be misleading to suggest that all psychologists since that time have accepted without question the idea of localisation. Several alternative theories have been proposed this century, including Lashley's principles of mass action (that the entire cortex is involved in all functions), and equipotentiality (that each cortical region can assume control for any given behaviour).

Lashley's ideas can be traced back to the work of Flourens that I mentioned earlier, and like him, Lashley used lesion and ablation techniques, and worked exclusively with animals. Many of his studies measured the effects of brain lesions on speed of maze learning in rodents. He would remove a small region of brain, then, following a period of recovery, see how quickly the animal could learn to find a food pellet at the end of a maze. On the basis of many such trials, Lashley concluded that the amount of lesioned brain tissue rather than its location best predicted how poorly the rat would do in the maze, supporting his idea of mass action.

However, his findings could also be used to support localisation of function. Think for a moment about the information a rat might use to run the maze and find the food. Presumably this could include visual information, tactile information and smell, in addition to any more sophisticated concepts such as sense of direction, distance travelled and so on. Indeed, effective maze learning probably depends on the integration of all this information. When Lashley 'lesioned' different bits of brain, he might have interfered with the animal's tactile skills or sense of smell, whilst leaving other functions intact. The animal could still learn the maze using the 'localised' functions that remained, although not as quickly as before.

Sound experimental support for Lashley's ideas has been hard to come by, and it is probably helpful to know that most psychologists continue to favour some form of localisation. Indeed, at present, the main questions in this area of psychology are less to do with *whether or not* the human cortex is organised locally, than the *extent* to which localisation of function applies, and whether it applies equally on both the left and right sides of the brain. Research into the concept of asymmetry of function has produced very interesting findings and this is reviewed in Chapter 4.

Distributed control

Today, most psychologists think that the human brain operates on the basis of (some form of) **distributed control**. Although this sounds rather complicated, think of it as meaning that psychological functions (such as language or movement) depend on the activity of, and connections between, several different but specific locations. Clearly, this is a different idea to the strict localisation of function concept mentioned earlier, but it is also quite distinct from Lashley's ideas of mass action and equipotentiality. In a way, it is a compromise between both ideas, because it implies some cortical specialisation (localisation of function) but also suggests that several interconnected centres may be involved in mediating function or behaviour. Today, the concept of distributed control, in which various discrete locations are interconnected to have overall collective responsibility for particular psychological functions, is seen again and again. Later in this book we consider the different networks of neurons that underpin movement as well as language and perception.

a) Identify two distinguishing features of Broca's, Wernicke's and conduction aphasia. Write a sentence about each feature.
b) How is work on aphasia used to support a distributed control model of cortical function?

Review exercise

Summary

Scientific interest in the relationship between brain structure and function can be traced back to the work of the nineteenth-century European neurologists. In the intervening 150 years, researchers have debated the extent to which the brain operates on the basis of localisation of function, or according to the principles of equipotentiality and mass action. Today, most psychologists working in this field think that some form of localisation involving distributed control best accounts for our current understanding of brain–behaviour relationships.

Further reading

Gazzaniga, M.S., Ivry, R.B. and Mangun, G.R. (1998) *Cognitive Neuroscience: the biology of the mind*, Norton: London, chapter 1. A beautifully illustrated historical account of early discoveries in neurology and physiology that shaped thinking about, and research into, brain–behaviour relationships.

Kolb, B. and Whishaw, I.Q. (1996) *Fundamentals of Human Neuropsychology*, 4th edn, Freeman: New York, chapter 1. An interesting and concise introduction to early research and theories in the area that we today call 'neuropsychology'.

2

The structure
of the brain

Introduction

In this chapter, we consider the structure of the human brain. We
know that, like other parts of the nervous system, the brain is made
up of many different types of nerve cell. The brain has been described
as the most complicated structure known to man. It therefore makes
sense to divide it up into separate regions, each of which is briefly
considered in turn. Since this book is about cortical functions, the
cortex will be given special consideration. This structure is the outer
surface of the brain, and in evolutionary terms is the most recently
developed region. It too is usually divided up, firstly in terms of left or
right side, and then, in relation to the bones of the skull, into lobes. As
you will see, cortical lobes can also be distinguished in terms of the
psychological functions they mediate.

The neuron hypothesis

As mentioned in Chapter 1, the brain looks solid, even when viewed through one of the low-magnification microscopes available last century. However, even 100 years ago nerves elsewhere in the body were known to be 'separate cells' rather than one massive branching structure. Since they connected with the spinal cord, which in turn connected to the brain, it raised the possibility that the brain too was made up of individual cells.

Confirmation depended on the development of techniques to improve the effectiveness (the definition) of microscopy. These coincided with the chance discovery that brain tissue could be stained, and that different stains highlighted different types of tissue. The most famous development in this area was the discovery in 1875 by the Italian researcher Golgi that certain brain cells could be stained by chemicals containing silver. The stained cells took on a dark appearance and were much easier to see under the microscope. Now the micro-structure of the brain could be examined.

Golgi's technique, which is still used today, led him to propose that the brain was actually a continuous mass of interconnected tissue (a little like a three-dimensional road-map). This type of structure had already been identified in the nervous system of spiders, and was known as a **nerve net**. Golgi's staining technique was adopted by the Spanish researcher (and academic rival of Golgi) Ramon y Cajal. He was able to show that the mammalian brain was not simply a massive nerve net, but actually comprised separate individual cells or **neurons**.

In other research, Cajal showed that neurons convey information around the nervous system (and brain) in the form of minute electrical impulses, which we now call 'nerve impulses' or '**action potentials**'. He was however unable to solve the puzzle as to how one neuron communicated with another. The discovery of chemical **synaptic transmission** was made by Otto Loewi in 1933 (see Loewi 1960), although our understanding of the exact mechanisms of synaptic functions is still incomplete.

Neurons and glia

We now know that our entire nervous system is made up of two fundamentally different classes of cell; neurons and **glial cells**.

Neurons are responsible for conveying nerve impulses around the nervous system, and communicating, via synaptic transmission, with other neurons, or in the periphery, with muscles. It is important to realise that neurons themselves do not move, but they can convey nerve impulses (action potentials) along their length very efficiently and quickly. The adult human brain contains about 10,000,000,000,000 neurons! (See Figure 2.1a.)

Yet glial cells (sometimes called neuroglia, or just glia) outnumber neurons 10 to 1! They play a range of vital supporting roles, but are not directly involved in either conveying nerve impulses or synaptic transmission. For example, in the brain, one type of glial cell (known as an oligodendrocyte) literally wraps itself around the 'cable' part of a neuron (the axon), rather like a carpet is wrapped round a central cardboard tube, to provide a sort of insulation known as a **myelin sheath**. Schwann cells do a similar job in other parts of the nervous system. Another type (known as microglia) can move around the nervous system, and they act rather like vacuum cleaners, removing (and digesting) dead or damaged tissue. (See Figure 2.1b.)

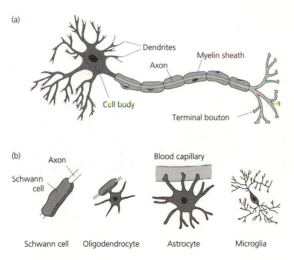

Figure 2.1 **Cells of the nervous system**
Source: Figure 2.1b: Kalat (1995), Reprinted with permission of Wadsworth Publishing, a division of International Publishing.

Notes:
(a)   The main components of a neuron.
(b)   Different types of glial cell.

As with glial cells, there are a variety of different types of neuron, some of which are found throughout the nervous system, and others which are only found in very discrete locations. For example, **amacrine cells** are found only in the part of the eye known as the retina, whereas **interneurons** (which acts as relays between other neurons) are widespread throughout the brain and spinal cord. However, because most neurons carry nerve impulses and engage in synaptic transmission it is helpful (though not entirely accurate) to think of them as all working in the same way.[1]

Developmental and ageing aspects

By now, you may have begun to wonder where all these cells come from and how they end up where they are. The answer to the first question is straightforward. Like all cells in our body, neurons and glia result from cell division, ultimately traceable back to the single fertilised egg which begins to divide shortly after conception. The second part of the question is, with a few exceptions, presently unanswerable, except that, during development, cells migrate (move), divide, and in certain cases selectively die. The neurons and glia remaining are our nervous system.

One thing we can be sure of is that the maximum number of neurons an individual ever has reaches a peak relatively early in life, and there is little evidence of further neuronal growth after the age of two. The fact that most neurons are already present explains (in part) why a newborn baby's head is large in comparison with the rest of its body.

The number of neurons remains static throughout childhood, but in adolescence begins to decline. It has been estimated that from the age of 15 or so onwards, humans lose about 15,000 neurons every day, which are not replaced. This works out to about 600 per hour, or 10 per minute! This apparently alarming figure must be set aside the vast number you start off with. If you consider a lifespan of 75 years, and use the figures I have given, you will find that the percentage loss of neurons at age 75 is no more than 3% of the total, assuming a normal

---

1 These processes are elegantly described in Kevin Silber's book, *The Physiological Basis of Behaviour*, in this series and need not be repeated here.

healthy life. Accelerated cell loss is, of course, a feature of several neurological disorders including **Alzheimer's** and **Parkinson's diseases**.

Unlike neurons, glial cells do increase in number throughout childhood and adolescence, and even in adulthood. In the **corpus callosum** (a structure in the middle of the brain that I describe later in this chapter), the amount of myelination increases (i.e. more oligodendrocytes form myelin sheaths) each year, with the structure only reaching full maturity at about 18 years. Incidentally, on a more sinister note, most brain tumours arise as a result of uncontrolled division of glial cells; not neurons.

Before we leave the issue of life-span changes, it is important to realise that for a nervous system to work effectively, it is not just the number of neurons which is important, but how they interconnect with each other. Recall from my earlier discussion that neurons communicate through (predominantly) chemical synapses. Although the absolute number of neurons declines with age from adolescence onwards, the number of connections or synapses between neurons *can increase*, and certainly does not necessarily follow the declining neuron count.

When there is brain damage, loss of cells may be compensated for by the formation of new synapses. In Parkinson's disease, which involves the loss of particular neurons, it is not until about three-quarters of these cells have died that the symptoms appear. Researchers think that in the period of disease prior to symptom onset, the remaining healthy cells form new synapses onto target cells, in effect replacing the inputs from the neurons that have died.

In the human brain, it has been estimated that the average neuron (not that any such thing exists) receives at least 1000 converging inputs, and can in turn, influence about the same number of neurons via its dividing axon (**divergence**). For some neurons whose role is to control the activity levels of others, the degree of divergence is such that a single neuron may synaptically influence at least a quarter of a million other neurons!

Dividing up the nervous system

Because the nervous system stretches from the top of your head to the tip of your toes, it makes sense to divide it up into more manageable chunks. I have already used the term central nervous system (CNS), and this is usually contrasted with **peripheral nervous system** (PNS). For mammals, the CNS is the brain and spinal cord, and the PNS is everything else. Sometimes it is useful to further sub-divide the peripheral nervous system into the branch in which neurons carry nerve impulses to voluntary muscles (i.e. ones you can consciously control), and the branch carrying nerve impulses to muscles such as the heart and gut, which are not under voluntary control. The former is referred to as the **skeletal nervous system** and the latter is the **autonomic nervous system** (ANS).

Another way of sub-dividing the nervous system is to take into account the direction of nerve impulses conveyed along particular neurons. **Afferent or sensory neurons** carry nerve impulses towards the brain. **Efferent or motor neurons** carry impulses from the brain outwards towards muscles.

A further useful distinction differentiates neurons with and without myelin sheaths. The sheath, (which actually only covers the axon part of the neuron), dramatically improves speed of conduction, allowing nerve impulses to be carried at over 100 metres per second. The myelin gives these neurons a characteristic pinky-white appearance; hence the term **white matter**. Unmyelinated neurons convey action potentials much more slowly, and have a pinky-grey appearance. So too do cell bodies, giving rise to the term **grey matter**.

Since we are in the business of defining terms, I will add a few more into the pot. Quite often, cell bodies of neurons will be clumped together in one location. (They don't actually touch one another but lie in close proximity to each other). These clumps are known as **ganglia** or **nuclei**. Similarly, the cable parts of neurons (the axons) often run side by side, from one part of the nervous system to another. Once again, they don't actually merge into a single structure, but they do lie next to each other. Bundles of axons are known as **tracts** or **nerves**. It is important to remember just how small and densely packed axons can be. For example, the optic nerve, which we will be considering in more detail in Chapter 7, is made up exclusively of myelinated axons. In humans, it is about the same diameter as a piece of cooked spaghetti, yet it comprises the axons of over two million individual retinal cells, conveying information, in the form of nerve impulses, from the retina into the brain.

The central nervous system (CNS)

In mammals, the CNS includes all nerve tissue which is encased in bone (see Figure 2.2.) Although this book is concerned with the cortex and its functions, it is important to realise that the cortex itself is only one part of the brain. Thus for completeness, we will briefly consider other elements of the CNS too. If you are not interested in the anatomy of the rest of the brain or spinal cord, skip to the section headed 'Cortex'.

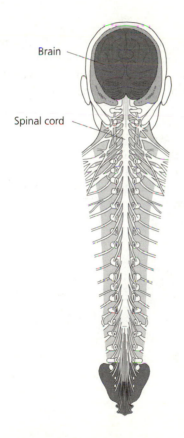

Brain

Spinal cord

Figure 2.2   **The human central nervous system**

The spinal cord

The spinal cord nestles within the vertebrae, and is made up of both grey and white matter. The grey matter comprises, for the most part, unmyelinated interneurons. The white matter surrounds the central grey matter, and comprises vast pathways or tracts of myelinated axons conveying both afferent and efferent information. Some of these tracts run the entire length of the spinal cord although any given neuron only carries information in one direction.

The brain stem

This comprises the medulla, pons and cerebellum. The medulla is the lowest region of the brain, and, in addition to the pathways from the spinal cord, contains a series of regions that control basic vegetative processes such as respiration, heart rate and certain reflexes. **Brain death** is assessed by the absence of electrical activity in this lowest region of the brain. (See Figure 2.3.)

The pons lies just above the medulla on the front of the brain stem. It is the main link between the cerebellum and the rest of the brain. It also has a role in certain aspects of both visual and auditory processing, and, amongst other things, helps to co-ordinate eye movements in relation to balance. (See Figure 2.3.)

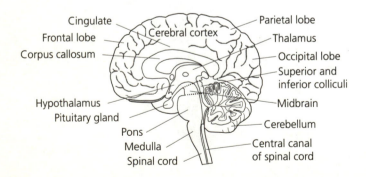

Figure 2.3   **Sagittal section through the human brain**

The cerebellum is the large 'walnut'-like structure on the back part of the brain stem roughly at the level of the ears (see Figure 2.3). Amongst other functions, this structure is concerned with the learning and control of skilled movements, particularly those 'enacted' through time, in other words, skills such as playing a piano or performing some complex gymnastic routine, in which the sequence of controlling muscles has to be precisely co-ordinated. People who have incurred damage to their cerebellum often appear drunk, even to the point of slurring their speech, which after all, depends on the co-ordination (in time) of muscles in the throat and mouth.

The midbrain

Here, we would find the thalamus, the hypothalamus, and four little bumps on the back of the brain stem above the cerebellum . The bottom two (the inferior colliculi) are concerned with auditory processing, and especially in turning the head towards an auditory stimulus. The top two (the superior colliculi) do a similar job, but for visual processing. (See Figure 2.3.)

The hypothalamus is involved in controlling behaviours that help the body maintain an equilibrium or satisfy its needs. It will be no surprise to learn that it is the nerve centre (no pun intended) for the control of eating, drinking and temperature regulation. It also includes control regions for the autonomic nervous system, and, in collaboration with the pituitary gland, helps to co-ordinate much of the endocrine (hormone) system. (See Figure 2.3.)

The thalamus is a relay station for sensory information coming into the brain, and for much motor output leaving it. By relay station, I mean that sensory information (from a particular modality such as vision) enters the thalamus, or more specifically a particular nucleus of it, where it may undergo some processing, before being sent on to a particular region of cortex for further detailed analysis.

The basal ganglia and limbic system

Two other systems of neurons need mention at this point. The basal ganglia comprise not one but several interconnected structures (the caudate, putamen, globus pallidus and substantia nigra). (See Figure

2.4.) Whilst it is not necessary to remember their names, it is helpful to have an idea of how this network of structures collectively helps to control movement. The basal ganglia do not, for example, initiate or terminate movement in isolation. Rather, in combination with the motor cortex, they determine which possible actions actually get put into effect, by permitting some and inhibiting others. The basal ganglia serve as a sort of gate-keeper for motor plans which originate in the cortex, and damage to any of the component structures (or the pathways which interconnect them) will impair the co-ordination or control of movement.

The limbic system also comprises several different interconnected structures, including the hippocampus, amygdala, septum and hypo-thalamus. It is, in certain respects, the *emotional* equivalent of the *motor* basal ganglia. In other words, activity in the limbic system adds emotional tone (fear, anger, pleasure) to behaviour. Like the basal ganglia, the limbic system seems not to work in isolation, but rather in collaboration with both lower (brain stem) and higher (cortical) brain centres. Damage or abnormal functioning in the limbic system is asso-

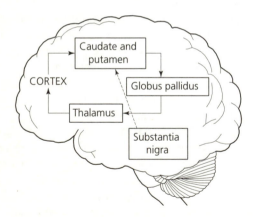

Figure 2.4 **Schematic diagram of some components of the basal ganglia (not to scale)**

Note: The main input to the basal ganglia comes from the frontal lobes of the cortex. The main output (via the thalamus) is back to the cortex. The substantia nigra controls the overall activity of this loop.

Identify the location of each of the following structures, and comment on their behavioural role(s).

a) cerebellum
b) medulla
c) basal ganglia
d) limbic system
e) hypothalamus
f) thalamus

ciated with inappropriate emotional responding, and may be related to certain psychiatric disorders including schizophrenia, depression and anxiety. Both of these systems are conventionally regarded as forebrain structures.

The cortex

When you look at a human brain, you can see the brain stem, the cerebellum and cortex. (See Figure 2.7.) The cortex seems to cover much of the rest of the brain, although it is actually a forebrain (front) structure. It has a bumpy folded appearance. The bumps are called gyri (singular: **gyrus**), and the folds or indents are called sulci (singular: **sulcus**). Gyri and sulci dramatically increase the surface area of the cortex. In fact, about two-thirds of cortical tissue is hidden in these folds. If you could flatten out the human cortex, it would cover a square measuring about 50 cm $\times$ 50 cm.

Cortex means bark and it is a very apt term in this case, for the cortex is only a few millimetres thick. Its pinky grey appearance tells us that it is made up primarily of cell bodies (remember cell bodies do not have myelin sheaths), which are usually arranged in a series of between four and six layers parallel to the surface. Immediately underneath, the appearance changes to white, indicating vast tracts of myelinated neuron axons conveying information to and from the cortex (via the thalamus), and between one cortical region and another.

Like many other brain structures the cortex is often described as being *bilaterally symmetrical*: this means that the left and right sides are like mirror images of each other. However, as I will show in Chapter 4 this is only approximately true, and several important anatomical distinctions between left and right side are apparent on closer inspection. The two sides of the cortex are sometimes referred to as hemispheres, and again the term is apt: taken as a whole, the cortex looks a little like a partly inflated ball. However, it is important to note that strictly speaking each hemisphere actually contains many sub-cortical structures as well.

The hemispheres are connected to each other by a number of pathways, of which the largest by far is the corpus callosum. This structure is actually a massive band of axons running from one side of the cortex to the other. Although it is only about 10 cm long and no more than 1 cm in thickness, it includes over 200,000,000 myelinated axons! The relative isolation of the two hemispheres is best demonstrated by the observation that it is possible to insert a thin probe at any point along the longitudinal fissure (which separates them) and the first thing you would touch is the corpus callosum about 2 to 3 cm down. (See Figure 2.5.)

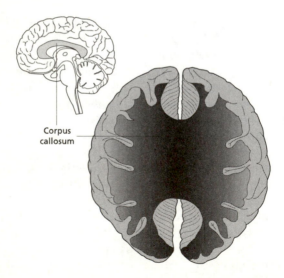

Corpus callosum

Figure 2.5 **The corpus callosum**

Source: Kalat (1995: 489, Figure 14.1). Reprinted with permission of Wadsworth Publishing, a division of International Publishing.

I mentioned earlier that the cortex itself is made up primarily of cell bodies, and one of the largest and most prominent types of cortical cell is the so-called pyramidal cell. (See Figure 2.6.) This type of neuron has a very extensive branch-like structure. The branches are known as dendrites, and are the part of neuron most likely to receive inputs from other neurons. Under a microscope these pyramidal cells look a little like Christmas trees, with the top branches corresponding to dendrites, and the lower broader part comprising a cell body and further sideways pointing dendrites. The stem and roots of the tree would be the axon, which leaves the cortex to form a strand of white matter. Pyramidal cells are oriented at 90° to the surface of the cortex, and clusters of these cells are sometimes called columns. (As we shall see, a regular feature of cortical organisation is its so-called column structure).

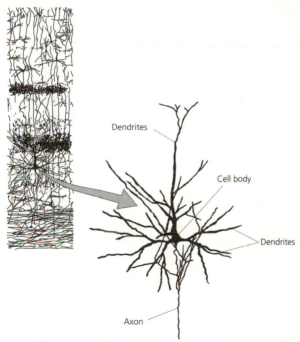

Figure 2.6   **The layers of the cortex and a pyramidal cortical neuron**

Source: Adapted from Rosenzweig *et al.* (1996: 63). Reprinted with permission from Sinauer Associates, Sunderland, MA.

Sensory, motor and association cortex

Another way of distinguishing between different parts of the cortex has, historically, been according to function. Some (discrete) cortical regions clearly have primary sensory or motor responsibilities. Other (more extensive) regions don't, and the term *association cortex* has been used for many years as a 'catch-all' for these cortical areas. Yet research shows that relatively little associating (or combining) of sensory input actually takes place here! It seems that most of the association cortex is actually involved in what amounts to a more elaborate (or 'higher-order') processing of information. For example, the primary visual cortex deals with sensory registration, whilst regions of visual association cortex are concerned with colour perception, object recognition and movement … amongst other things. (See chapter 7.)

The lobes of the cortex

Another way of identifying cortical regions is in relation to the skull bones that they lie under. We differentiate between four lobes; eight if you include both hemispheres. Not only can the lobes be distinguished by their anatomical location, they also separate to some

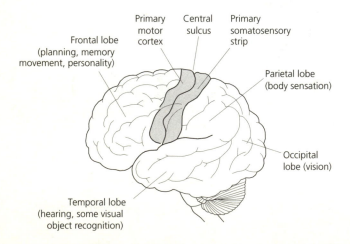

Figure 2.7   **The lobes of the cortex**

extent in terms of the psychological processes that they are concerned with. (See Figure 2.7.)

The frontal lobes

If you think of the human brain as looking a little like a boxing glove from the side, then the frontal lobes comprise the part of the glove that the fingers would occupy. They comprise about 30% of the entire complement of brain cells, and are the part of the cortex that is more highly developed (evolved?) in humans than any other primate. At one time, the main function of these lobes was thought to be that of controlling movement. However, as we have learned more about them, it has become clear that in addition to their key role in movement, they are also involved in planning, generating ideas, language, **working memory**, and personality. A glance at these functions shows why some psychologists think of the frontal lobes as the cortical region that, above all others, defines humanity.

I describe the role of the frontal lobes in movement in Chapter 5. However, one of the earliest and most vivid illustrations of their role in personality was the case of Phineas Gage. He worked as a labourer for an American railway company, and his job was to blast rock to make tunnels and cuttings. He had to tamp dynamite into bore holes using a long tamping rod, and lay charges. One day, something went wrong, and his three foot long and one inch wide tamping rod was propelled by the explosion through his cheek and out of the top of his head at about 800 miles per hour. The tamping rod effectively removed (ablated) much of the front part of his left frontal lobe. Although Phineas made a full recovery from the mishap, his personality changed completely. Having previously been known as a man of integrity and decency, he became fitful, vulgar, irreverent, and prone to let his animal passions get the better of him, and anyone else who happened to be around! The case of Phineas Gage, along with countless other well documented cases of localised frontal damage, confirms the role of the frontal lobes in helping to shape personality.

The parietal lobes

The parietal lobes are located immediately behind the frontal lobes, and are separated from them by the central sulcus which is a deep groove running across the top of the brain (roughly from ear to ear). These lobes have important sensory functions, especially in relation to touch and vision, which I describe in some detail in Chapters 5 and 7.

The first strip of parietal lobe (the furthest forward gyrus if you like) is the primary somatosensory cortex. Neurons here respond to touch sensation from very distinct body regions, and the entire body is 'mapped' onto this cortical strip. For example, touch receptors in your right hand will send nerve impulses that end up in your left primary somatosensory strip. Different adjacent columns of neurons here will respond to input from each finger (and each part of each finger!).

Further back (i.e. further away from the central sulcus), more posterior regions of parietal lobe are involved in more 'integrative' sensory functions, linking for example, touch with visual information or with memory. Damage here can lead to a disorder known as **astereognosis**, which is marked by the inability to recognise objects by touch.

The occipital lobes

The left and right occipital lobes are tucked behind and underneath the parietal lobes at the back of the cortex and they deal with visual input. Some areas are concerned with the perception of form, others with movement and still others with colour. I describe these attributes in considerable detail in Chapter 7. Damage here almost always results in some impairment to vision, and can lead to **cortical blindness**. For example, extensive damage to just the right occipital lobe will result in blindness in the left visual field (everything to the left of centre as you look straight ahead).

The temporal lobes

In my boxing-glove analogy, the temporal lobe would be the thumb (except you have one on each side). The front part of this lobe is separated from the frontal lobe (which it lies to the side of), but the rear (posterior) sections are bounded by the parietal and occipital lobes, and the actual boundaries are not clearly defined by sulci.

The upper region of the temporal lobe is the primary auditory cortex, input coming mainly from the ear on the opposite side of the body. On the left side, adjacent regions, especially behind the primary auditory cortex, are involved in the recognition of language sounds. On the right side, the equivalent regions are involved in interpreting non-verbal speech sounds such as tone, rhythm, and emotion.

However, the temporal lobes are not concerned just with auditory processing. Lower (inferior) regions for example are involved in visual object recognition. In general, cells towards the front of the temporal

Try to identify cortical locations that may lead to the following behavioural impairments:

a) inability to recognise an object by touch
b) marked change in personality
c) failure to interpret the emotional tone of a verbal message
d) blindness in the left visual field

Review exercise

lobes respond only to very specific visual stimuli such as faces, or types of animal, suggesting that stored memories of items may be located here.

Summary

The brain, like other parts of the nervous system, is made up of neurons and glial cells. Neurons alone carry nerve impulses around the nervous system. To begin to understand how the brain works, it makes sense to divide it up, and the various component parts of the hindbrain, midbrain and forebrain have been introduced. It is also helpful to divide up the cortex, and the structure and function(s) of each lobe have been reviewed. No matter how many times I describe the brain to students, I still marvel at the sheer complexity of it, and I hope you share my sense of wonder. I am also amazed that such a complicated structure goes wrong so infrequently. However, as we have already seen, brain damage, disorder and disease, when it does occur, can sometimes shed considerable light on the functioning of the normal intact brain.

Further reading

Carlson, N.R. (1994) *Physiology of Behaviour*, 5th edn, London: Allyn & Bacon. Another excellent physiological psychology textbook, pitched at a more advanced level than Kalat. Less 'colour', but more detail.

Kalat, J.W. (1998) *Biological Psychology*, 6th edn, Pacific Grove: Brooks & Cole. The definitive introductory textbook in physiological psychology. Up to date, comprehensive, and superbly illustrated, with very helpful summaries, and quizzes and questions to challenge the reader throughout.

Silber, K. (1999) *The Physiological Basis of Behaviour*, Routledge: London (this series). The companion book to this text; concise, readable, and pitched at a similar level, but with a focus on the functioning of nervous and endocrine systems.

3

Methods in neuropsychology

Introduction
Techniques of measurement of brain structure and function
Neuropsychological assessment
Summary

Introduction

In this chapter, I introduce some of the methods that researchers use to explore the relationships between brain structure and function. I start with a brief review of classic techniques, many of which have been used by scientists for some considerable time. Next I identify some of the in-vivo techniques which allow researchers to visualise the structure and/or functioning of the 'living' brain. I conclude this chapter with an illustration of an exciting application of in-vivo imaging in psychiatry.

Techniques of measurement of brain structure and function

Until quite recently, the options for measurement of brain structure and function have been rather limited. Structural analysis depended on **biopsy**, or **post-mortem**. The former is a drastic technique involving the removal and analysis of small (but irreplaceable) samples of brain tissue. It relies on a somewhat hit and miss technique (of removing tissue from the 'appropriate' area of brain). The latter requires the subject to be dead, so that early signs of disease are likely to be masked by changes that occur as the disease progresses.

Sometimes, there are obvious signs of damage. For example, the brain of a person who has died as a result of **Huntington's chorea** or Alzheimer's disease will clearly look abnormal even to the naked eye. It may appear shrunken inwards from the skull. The gyri (bumps) will look 'deflated', and the sulci (grooves) will be wider.

Usually however, researchers are less interested in the outward appearance of the brain than in its cell structure and connectivity, perhaps within a discrete region. Staining techniques have enabled researchers to identify small groups of neurons, or even individual neurons using a light microscope. Microscopy has, of course developed considerably in the last 100 years, and today electron microscopes can produce images of individual synapses (junctions between neurons), or even of receptor sites on the surface of neurons for neurotransmitter chemicals.

Lesion and ablation

A long-standing technique in neurology has been to observe the effects of lesion (cutting) or ablation (removal) of nerve tissue. Lashley, for example, put forward the theory of mass action (which I introduced in Chapter 1) on the basis of lesion studies with animals. For obvious reasons these procedures are not used experimentally on humans (!), but sometimes brain tissue is removed for medical reasons, such as the removal of a tumour. Occasionally, surgical lesioning is also undertaken. (You will learn about the effects of lesioning the corpus callosum which brings about the 'split brain syndrome' in Chapter 4).

It is also possible to induce temporary lesions by administering a localised anaesthetic. The **Wada test** (Wada and Rasmussen; 1960) which involves administration of a fast-acting barbiturate to one hemisphere at a time, via the left or right carotid artery, is one such example.

Electrical stimulation

Much of the pioneering work on mapping out the primary somatosensory and motor cortex was done by the neurosurgeon Wilder Penfield. (e.g.; Penfield and Boldrey 1958). His subjects were recruited from amongst his patients, many of whom required surgery for life-threatening conditions such as removal of brain tumours or blood clots. He asked them whether, in the course of surgery, they would mind if he applied a mild stimulating electrode to the surface of their brains. His patients would not have been discomforted because the brain does not contain pain receptors. Moreover, quite a lot of brain surgery is conducted with the patient awake, so Penfield could talk to his subjects as he stimulated different parts of their exposed brains! Using this technique, Penfield was the first researcher to discover the amazing topographic representation of body areas in the primary motor and somatosensory cortex. (I describe this in detail in Chapter 5.)

Electrical recording

Penfield's technique involved the stimulation of neuronal tissue with very fine electrodes. We can also learn about brain function by recording its electrical activity. In Electroencephalography (EEG) and the closely related procedure of event-related potential (ERP) recording, electrodes are attached to the scalp, and the amplified electrical activity detected by them is displayed on a chart recorder. Often, several separate channels of EEG, corresponding to electrodes in different positions on the head, are recorded simultaneously. This procedure has proved invaluable in the diagnosis of epilepsy, and in the identification of sleep-related disorders. (See Figure 3.1.)

For ERP recording, a series of stimuli such as tones or light flashes are presented to the subject, and the raw EEG for a 1 or 2 second period following each stimulus is fed into a computer where it is summed and averaged. The idea is that there will be a response, or *event-related potential*, in the brain to each separate stimulus, although this may be small in comparison to the background EEG. By summing all the EEGs together and averaging them, the more-or-less random EEG is removed, to leave an ERP which has a characteristic waveform when shown on the computer screen. Various

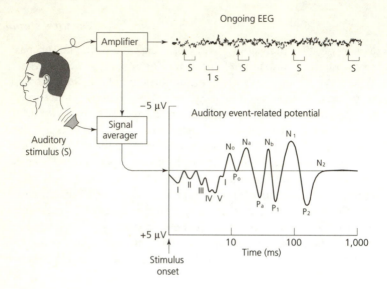

Figure 3.1 **Electrical recording of the brain: EEG and ERPs**

Source: Hillyard and Kutas (1983) . Reprinted, with permission, from the *Annual Review of Psychology*, Vol. 34 ©1983, by Annual Reviews www.annualreviews.org

Notes: The ongoing electroencephalography (EEG) (top) is recorded on the scalp through an amplifier. Every time a stimulus occurs (denoted by 'S' in the ongoing EEG), the electrical signal is recorded for a discrete period (e.g. 1 second). Signals from all such time periods are then averaged because ERPs are too small to be detected in the ongoing EEG. The resulting ERP waveform to an auditory stimulus is shown below.

abnormalities in this waveform have been linked to predisposition to alcoholism and schizophrenia. The ERP technique has also proved useful in assessing disorders of attention.

Recently, a further variant of ERP known as magnetoencephalography (MEG) has been developed. (See Mogilner *et al.*'s study of re-mapping in the cortex in Chapter 8.) This technique, which requires upwards of 60 electrodes to be attached to the subject's head, takes advantage of the fact that when neurons are active, they generate tiny magnetic fields. MEG can locate the source of maximum magnetic field activity in response to stimuli, and map these areas in real time. The computer output actually resembles a colour-coded 'wave' of activity, sweeping through the brain regions that are responding to the stimulus. This technique has proved useful in identifying the precise focal origins of epileptic seizures.

Give one example of each of the following 'techniques', and explain what we have learned from this procedure:

a) staining
b) lesioning
c) ablation
d) electrical stimulation
e) electrical recording

Progress exercise

In-vivo imaging

Since the mid-1970s, several 'in-vivo' imaging techniques have been developed. The common feature of these procedures is that researchers can produce images of the structure or functional activity of the brains of *living* people. (See Figure 3.2.) PET scans (positron emission tomography) can provide colour-coded images of a person's brain as s/he undertakes different sorts of task: reading words, solving mental arithmetic, listening to music, and so on.

The technique takes advantage of the fact that active neurons use more glucose (fuel). Shortly before the scan, a small amount of radioactively labelled glucose is given to the subject by injection, some of which will be taken up by active neurons. By using a scanner that can detect emitted radioactivity, the activity level of different regions of the brain can then be assessed. PET is therefore a powerful means of assessing *functional* activity in different brain regions, although it cannot be used to identify subtle changes to brain structure. I illustrate an exciting application of PET to mapping language areas by Raichle and his colleagues in Chapter 8.

(a) Computerised tomography (CT)

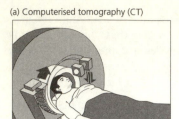
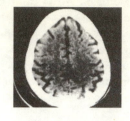

(b) Magnetic resonance imaging (MRI)

(c) Positron emission tomography (PET)

Figure 3.2 **Some in-vivo imaging procedures**

Source: Rosenzweig *et al.* (1996: 66). Reprinted with permission from Sinauer Associates, Sunderland, MA.

Notes: The procedures (left) and images obtained (right) from three important brain-imaging techniques.

(a)   A CT scan of a patient with Alzheimer's Disease. Note the 'shrunken' appearance of the brain, and wider sulci. (Courtesy of Bruce Moore, University of Liverpool)

(b)   A coronal section MRI scan. Note the clearly discernible ventricles and gyri. (Courtesy of Richard Hopkins, Withington Hospital, Manchester)

(c)   A horizontal PET scan of Richard Drake's brain. These are usually colour-enhanced by computer to show different levels of activation. (Thanks to Richard Drake, Withington Hospital, Manchester)

Computerised tomography (CT, but also known as CA(axial)T) on the other hand, provides a means of assessing brain structure, but not function. This was the first in-vivo technique to be developed, and works by passing very low levels of X-radiation through the subject's head at a series of different angles (through 180°). A computer analyses each pass, and generates what is, effectively, a compound X-ray. CT scans cannot measure functional activity but they have provided valuable information about *structural* changes seen in the brains of some people with dementia, and about the effects and location of brain damage in general.

More recently, magnetic resonance imaging (MRI) has also 'come on stream'. Initially, at least, MRI was introduced as a rival to CT. Scans provide photographic quality images of the brain, and the entire brain can be seen in successive slices by altering the position (and hence focal depth) of the scanner. The technique itself is incredibly complicated. (It relies on measurement of the response of neurons to radio waves in a very strong magnetic field!) However, a major advantage that it has over CT scanning is that it does not depend on radioactivity.

An exciting recent development of this technique known as functional magnetic resonance imaging (fMRI) permits simultaneous measurement of brain *structure* and *function*. Although fMRI has only been available for a short time, it has been adopted enthusiastically by researchers, because like MRI, fMRI scanning does not require the use of radioactive markers. Amongst many of its applications, it has recently been used to identify functional changes in frontal brain regions as subjects undertake tests of working memory (e.g. Wickelgren 1997).

Other in-vivo imaging procedures that you may read about include regional cerebral blood flow (rCBF) and single photon emission computerised tomography (SPECT). They are both variants on PET technology. In rCBF, the subject inhales a small amount of a radioactive gas such as xenon. This is absorbed into the blood, but does not react with it. It simply goes wherever the blood goes. The subject sits in a piece of apparatus which looks a little like the sort of dryer seen in hair salons! This has a series of sensors which can detect the radioactivity from the transported xenon, and since more blood is required by 'active' brain regions, a computer can build up an image of areas of greater (and lesser) activity based on the detection rates.

SPECT differs from PET in certain technical respects, the upshot of which is that the clarity of the scans is less precise because they take longer to generate.

Evaluation of in-vivo techniques

The development of in-vivo scanning marked the beginning of a new era in brain research. For the first time scientists could examine the structure or functioning of *the living brain*. It became possible to see exactly how extensive a patient's internal brain injury or damage was, and researchers could begin to do valuable brain research in individuals with 'intact' brains. By using special 'labelling' techniques it even became possible to observe for the first time where in the brain drugs were exerting their effects.

Despite the scientific advances that have been made as a result of the wider availability of CT, PET and MRI, there are drawbacks to each technique. Both PET and CT expose participants to radioactivity: X-rays in the case of CT, radioactive markers in the case of PET. Although the quantities are small, any exposure to radiation carries some risk. In the case of PET, the markers are a matter of concern for two practical reasons too. Firstly they are expensive. Secondly, they soon leave the body, which means that psychological measurements must be taken over only a short period of time. MRI and fMRI do not have these problems, and may soon replace CT and PET as the techniques are refined. However, even in the case of fMRI, there remains a problem in interpreting the output because it is presently impossible to say whether the hot-spots of activity that this technique reveals result from activation in excitatory neurons or inhibitory neurons!

Neuropsychological assessment

The neuropsychological approach relies on the use of tests that have been developed so that poor performance may be a sign of either focal (localised) or diffuse (widespread) brain damage. Usually, a series of tests (known as a test battery) will be given. One widely used battery is the Halstead–Reitan, which includes measures of verbal and non-verbal intelligence, language, tactile and manipulative skills, auditory sensitivity, and so on (Reitan and Wolfson 1993). Some of the tests are very straightforward: the Wisconsin card sort test requires respondents to match cards according to symbol shape, colour or number. The Corsi block-tapping test measures spatial memory using a series of strategically placed wooden blocks on a tray. A third test measures memory span for sets of digits. The Luria–Nebraska test battery (Luria 1966) is an even more exhaustive procedure taking two to three hours to administer, and including 269 test items. (See Figure 3.3.)

As I suggested, poor performance on one particular test may signal possible localised damage or dysfunction, whilst poor across-the-board performance may indicate generalised damage. For example as I mentioned in Chapter 2, inability to recognise objects by touch (astereognosis) is a sign of damage to the parietal lobes. A poor verbal test score (compared with a normal non-verbal test score) may indicate widespread left-hemisphere damage.

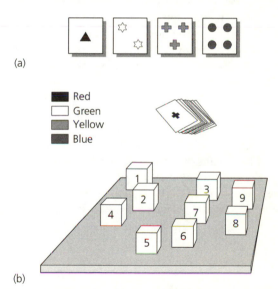

(a)

(b)

Figure 3.3 **Examples of neuropsychological tests**

Source: Adapted from (a) Milner (1963) and (b) Milner (1971).

Notes:

(a) the Wisconsin card sorting test

(b) Corsi's block-tapping board.

Evaluation of neuropsychological assessment

Neuropsychological testing has gained considerable respect in recent years. However, it would be wrong to think that a battery of neuropsychological tests alone could somehow provide the researcher or clinician with a complete map of brain functioning. At best they give an indication of underlying problems.

Two further concerns also merit consideration. First, an apparently normal performance on neuropsychological tests can be deceptive. We know that as individuals recover from brain damage, they often develop alternative strategies or techniques to overcome their deficits. A particularly powerful example of this process is the normal (or near normal) language function seen in adolescents who as children incurred severe left-hemisphere damage. Secondly, although neuropsychological and in-vivo assessments usually agree about what regions of brain are dysfunctional or damaged, they do not always, and the reasons for this are unclear.

Despite these concerns, researchers agree that the use of neuropsychological tests in combination with in-vivo techniques is potentially a very informative procedure. If a certain test is known to draw on the capacity of a particular brain region, the test could be given to a subject whilst s/he is being scanned. This combined technique has recently been used by Smith and Jonides (1994) to examine the role(s) of the frontal lobes in working memory. They selected various neuropsychological tests of verbal and non-verbal working memory, and recorded PET scans of normal subjects as they completed them. The results showed a clear division of labour: non-verbal working memory led to increased right frontal activation, whereas verbal working memory caused greater activation in the left frontal (and parietal) regions.

In-vivo imaging in psychiatry

I want to end this chapter with an example of one of the most remarkable and exciting applications of PET, as exemplified by the work of the psychologist Chris Frith and colleagues (see Silbersweig *et al.* 1995). They have used PET to measure brain activity in a group of mentally ill patients who were experiencing **hallucinations** *at the time* the scan was done. Preliminary results indicate that auditory hallucinations are linked to activation of particular regions of cortex, especially in the left temporal lobe, as well as parts of the left orbital region of the frontal lobe. Although it is still too early to say where, how, or why hallucinations form, the use of PET shows beyond doubt that the *experience* of hallucinations is related to changes in activity in various regions or cortex.

1. For each of the following in-vivo imaging procedures, identify their main strengths and weaknesses:

    a)   CT
    b)   PET
    c)   MRI

2. Why is the combination of neuropsychological testing and in-vivo imaging potentially such a powerful technique?

Review exercise

Summary

Researchers interested in understanding brain function and its relations to psychological function can now draw on a wide range of techniques. In this chapter I have introduced lesion and ablation, electrical stimulation and recording, and the in-vivo imaging procedures. Consideration is also given to the use of neuropsychological testing. Researchers have moved rapidly from an era in which analysis of brain structure could usually only be assessed after the person had died, to an era in which the various in-vivo imaging techniques are quickly becoming almost as commonplace as having an X-ray. In-vivo imaging is proving to be a particularly powerful research tool when used in tandem with other neuropsychological procedures.

Further reading

Kolb, B. and Whishaw, I.Q. (1996) *Fundamentals of Human Neuropsychology*, 4th edn, New York: Freeman & Co, chapter 26. A thorough introduction to neuropsychological assessment, with examples from the authors' own clinical casenotes and research.

Rosenzweig, M.R., Leiman, A.L. and Breedlove, S.M. (1996) *Biological Psychology*, Massachusetts: Sinauer Associates, chapter 2. Comprehensive and well-illustrated review of techniques in physiological psychology and neuroscience generally, including a concise review of in-vivo imaging techniques.

4

Lateralisation

Introduction

As I mentioned in Chapter 2, at first glance, the two cortical hemispheres look pretty much like mirror images of each other. Yet closer inspection reveals many subtle differences in structure. Behavioural studies suggest differences in function too. The study of **lateralisation** is the study of the distinct patterns of psychological functioning seen in the two hemispheres. Hemispheric specialisation is also sometimes known as **asymmetry of function** because of the different (asymmetric) responsibilities that psychologists have observed. In this chapter, we consider the various ways that scientists have examined this asymmetry, and the conclusions that they have drawn from their research.

Structural differences

The two hemispheres of the adult human brain are *not* mirror images of one another, and differ in a number of characteristic ways.

- Viewed from the top of the head, the right frontal lobe extends further forward, and the left occipital lobe further back.
- The dividing line between the frontal and temporal lobes (known as the Sylvian fissure) is longer and less sloped on the left side than the right.
- A region of temporal lobe adjacent to the Sylvian fissure is much larger on the left than the right. This area of cortex has been linked to language comprehension for at least 100 years.
- Cells in the region of left frontal lobe, which we now call Broca's area, have many more synaptic connections than the equivalent region in the right hemisphere.
- The area known as the angular gyrus (at the back of the parietal lobe), which may be important in reading, is larger on the left than the right side.
- The parietal area on the right side (just behind the location of the angular gyrus on the left) is larger and has more synaptic contacts. This region is linked with spatial processing.

Even at this level of analysis we begin to see a pattern suggesting links between structure and function, with the left hemisphere being concerned with linguistic and the right hemisphere with spatial skills. (See Figure 4.1.)

Neurological cases

Obviously we cannot manipulate brain damage experimentally in humans, but an alternative is to look at the brains of people who have suffered an accident or disease (neurological cases). In general terms, damage to the left hemisphere usually results in a greater impairment to linguistic function than to spatial (or non-linguistic) function, whereas the reverse is true for right hemisphere damage. However, we need to bear in mind that the degree and extent of damage is variable, and it is difficult to generalise on the basis of case studies alone.

A greater degree of control occurs where tissue must be surgically

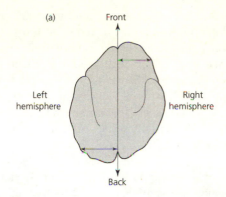

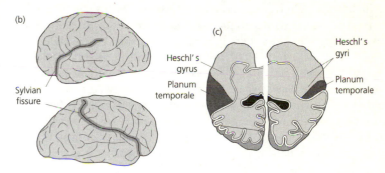

Figure 4.1 **Some asymmetries of the human brain**

Source: Kolb and Whishaw (1996). Reprinted with permission from Freeman & Co.

Notes:

(a) The right frontal region typically extends further forwards and is wider than the left frontal region, whereas for the occipital region the opposite is true: this region of the left hemisphere extends farther back and is wider.

(b) The Sylvian fissure extends farther horizontally in the left hemisphere (top), whereas in the right hemisphere (bottom), it takes more of an upward turn.

(c) The planum temporale, which can be clearly seen after the cortical tissue above the Sylvian fissure is removed, as is shown by the solid line in (b), is typically larger on the left than on the right.

removed. Taylor (1969) reported on two cases of patients who under-went temporal lobectomies (removal of temporal lobes) to remove brain tumours. Each patient completed a battery of neuropsycholog-ical and IQ tests before and after surgery. For the patient whose left temporal lobe was lesioned, there was a significant decline in performance on tasks with a verbal component, but no significant change in non-verbal function. For the patient who underwent a right temporal lobectomy, the exact reverse pattern of outcome was observed. Verbal skills were preserved, but spatial performance dipped markedly.

This pattern of distinct (opposite) impairment is referred to by psychologists as **double dissociation**, and is also observed in patients with left and right frontal and parietal lesions. Once again (in general terms) left-sided damage tends to impact more on verbally based skills, and right-sided damage on non-verbally based skills. For example, damage to the left frontal lobe usually leads to a decline in verbal fluency (*think of as many words beginning with the letter S as possible*), but not to design fluency (*draw as many patterns made of four lines as possible*). In general, right-sided damage is linked to impairments in a wide range of skills, including spatial orientation, discriminating tones, and face recognition. Left-sided damage is more likely to be associated with some loss of language function.

The split brain syndrome

Forty years ago, the drugs used to control epilepsy were not as effec-tive as those available today. For some people medications were unable to prevent regular epileptic seizures, making any semblance of a normal life impossible. At the same time, scientists were beginning to realise that the seizures themselves could cause progressive damage to the brain. Seizures often seem to originate in a particular location, but then spread (rather like ink on a blotter) to affect adjacent cortical regions. Sometimes, they pass via the corpus callosum to the opposite hemisphere. This structure was once thought to do little more than hold the two hemispheres together! However, as I described in Chapter 2, we know that it is made up of millions of myelinated axons carrying information from one hemisphere to the other. (See Figure 2.5.)

Having exhausted other treatments, two Californian surgeons,

Bogen and Vogel decided to try to contain seizure activity to just one hemisphere by lesioning the corpus callosa of their patients. All told, about 100 people underwent this procedure. Each was carefully monitored and assessed on a battery of psychological tests both before and after their operation. At first glance the procedure appeared remarkably effective. After a period of recovery, the intensity and frequency of epileptic activity was almost always reduced. Some patients no longer experienced major seizures at all! Moreover, in terms of psychological profile, patients' IQ scores, and scores on many other tests improved significantly, and, perhaps because of reduced seizure activity, most people claimed to feel better too.

These preliminary data presented a paradox to researchers. How could a surgical procedure which involved lesioning the major inter-hemispheric pathway not have a significant effect on psychological functioning? To address this question, a group of psychologists led by Sperry and Gazzaniga developed a series of tests which were designed to shed more light on the true nature of split brain syndrome.

Experimental studies

In order to understand the experimental procedures that Sperry, Gazzaniga and others developed it is important to know some basic physiology. Firstly, in higher mammals including humans, visual information from the right visual field (that is everything to your right if you look straight ahead) travels via the visual pathways to the left occipital lobe. Similarly, information from the left visual field travels to the right hemisphere. Secondly, the left hand is controlled by, and sends sensory information back to, the right hemisphere, and vice versa for the left hand. (See Figure 4.2.)

The researchers were interested to know what would happen if information was presented to the split brain patient one hemisphere at a time. Using a machine called a tachistoscope, they were able to present visual stimuli very briefly to either the left or right of a central fixation point on a screen in front of the patient. (The brief presentation allowed for recognition, but ensured that the individual did not have time to move his/her eyes towards the stimulus. Thus the image only entered one or other hemisphere). The subject had to say what (if anything) they had seen after each presentation. Sometimes, they were given the opportunity to reach behind a cloth screen, to feel

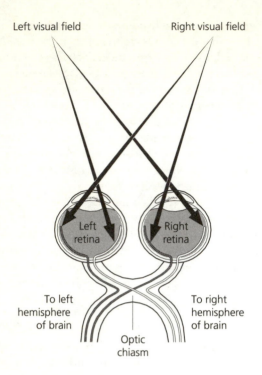

Figure 4.2 **Visual input to the two hemispheres**

Source: Kalat (1995: 187, figure 6.6). Reprinted with permission of
Wadsworth Publishing, a division of International Publishing.

items with either their left or right hand that might be related to the
stimuli presented on the screen.

Using this procedure the true nature of the split brain syndrome
was revealed. If a picture of a car was flashed to the right of the fixation point, the patient reported seeing a car. This would be expected
because the image travelled to the left (talking) hemisphere, and the
patient could say what s/he saw. If the same picture was flashed to the
left of the fixation point, the patient usually reported seeing nothing.
(The image had gone to the non-verbal right hemisphere.) However, if
the subject was then allowed to reach behind the screen with their left
hand, they could usually select a toy car from amongst other objects.

(Remember that the left hand connects to the right hemisphere.) Similarly, if the patient was allowed to 'doodle' with their left hand, a drawing of a car often appeared! Even more amazingly, when asked why they had drawn a car, patients usually expressed surprise and puzzlement, and were unable to give the right answer. (See Figure 4.3.)

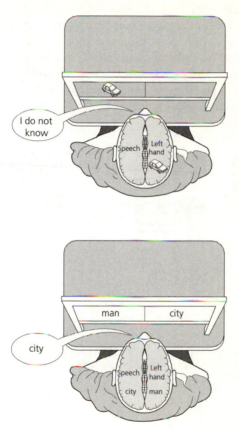

Figure 4.3 **Some illustrations of the split brain syndrome**

Notes: In the top illustration, the right hemisphere has seen the car but cannot access the name 'car' from the left hemisphere. In the bottom illustration, the left hemisphere responds with speech only to the word seen on the right of the screen.

In a related experiment Levy *et al.* (1972) flashed images made up of pairs of half-faces to his patients, again using a tachistoscope. For example one image comprised half the face of a girl on the left side, and half the face of an elderly man to the right. The fixation point was exactly on the joint at the bridge of the nose. When the subject was asked to say what they had seen, they reported seeing an intact (i.e. complete) picture of the man. We might have predicted this because this half image went to the left/talking hemisphere. However, when asked to select what they had seen from a set of complete pictures, split brain patients invariably chose the picture of the girl (which had gone to their right hemisphere). This observation has been used as evidence for the special dominant role of the right hemisphere in face recognition. (See Figure 4.4.)

Figure 4.4 **A split brain subject views chimeric figures**

Source: Levy *et al.* (1972). Reprinted with permission from Oxford University Press.

Notes:
(a) An example of a chimeric stimulus, composed of two half-faces, used with patients with split brain syndrome.
(b) When asked to indicate verbally which face was seen (a task under control of the left hemisphere), the patient names the child, whose picture was located in the right visual field. In such cases, accuracy is not high.
(c) When asked to use the left hand to point to the face that was seen (a task under control of the right hemisphere), the patient points to the picture that was in the left visual field. Under these conditions, accuracy is higher, a finding that indicates a right-hemisphere superiority for face-recognition processing.

The split brain syndrome and laterality

How do spilt brain patients deal with letters or words flashed to one or other hemisphere? The results of such studies are not quite as clear cut as we might expect. Gazzaniga and Hillyard (1971) reported that words presented to the right visual field could be read, and that objects corresponding to the word could be selected from behind a screen with the right (but not left) hand. However, although words presented to the left visual field (right hemisphere) could not usually be read aloud, some split brain patients could select related items with their left hand from behind the screen. This and other similar observations led to the claim that the right hemisphere also possessed language skills but was simply mute. However, careful investigation has confirmed that the linguistic capabilities of the right hemisphere are, for the most part, limited to concrete words, rather than to grammatical skills. Syntax (rules of grammar) is certainly restricted to the left hemisphere.

If the split brain studies support the idea of a key role for the left hemisphere in linguistic skills, do they tell us anything about any special roles and responsibilities of the right hemisphere? It seems that the right hemisphere is significantly better at spatial tasks such as route finding or jigsaw puzzles than the left. Some tests in the **Wechsler Adult Intelligence Scales (WAIS)** (Wechsler 1981) specifically address 'spatial' intelligence. If split brain subjects are given the block design test, which requires visual patterns to be copied using coloured blocks, they can do this much more effectively with their left hand (connected to the right hemisphere), than with their dominant right hand! (See Figure 7.4b.) In fact, performance with the right hand was little better than chance level.

The surgery which brings about the split brain syndrome effectively disconnects the two hemispheres. They are undamaged, but they can no longer communicate with one another. The effect highlights the specialisms of the two hemispheres that were also becoming apparent from other lines of enquiry: namely the key role of the left hemisphere for linguistic skills, and that of the right in spatial skills (including face perception). The amazing thing is that the surgery had so little effect on routine daily activities of split brain patients. Just occasionally, anecdotal accounts from individuals would indicate a degree of rivalry or disagreement between hemispheres (known as *hemispheric competition*). One woman complained that she went to select a dress from her wardrobe with her right hand, only to find her left hand reaching for a different one! On another occasion, the right hand turned the heating up, only for the left hand to turn it down again!

The reason why these events are few and far between is that in ordinary day-to-day activities, visual, auditory and most other sensory information actually finds it way into both hemispheres. It takes a cunning psychologist to think of situations in which input is restricted to just one! Patients themselves also learn strategies to ensure that sensory information gets to both hemispheres. One technique is to develop exaggerated head movements; a second is to make more use of *cross-cueing*. This is best illustrated by the following example: a split brain patient trying to identify a toothbrush by touch alone might drop it, or tweak the bristles; both of which may make sounds … which travel to both ears, and hence to both hemispheres.

Evaluation of split brain research

Despite the fascinating findings that have emerged from research with split brain subjects, a number of points should be born in mind when evaluating the data. Firstly, we should remember that the group of individuals who underwent the surgery could not be regarded as a normal or random sample. They were, in fact, a small group of people, who had suffered epilepsy for many years, and in the process, had usually been treated with a range of powerful drugs. Secondly, it is possible (actually probable) that their brains may have been affected by the repetitive seizures themselves. Thirdly, information about background IQ or other basic psychological abilities such as memory or attention is missing from many of the research reports. Overall, it is probably best to regard the evidence from individuals who have had split brain surgery as just one element in a search to establish the true nature of the different psychological specialisms of the two hemispheres.

Callosal agenesis

The split brain procedure was, of course, usually carried out on adults who had been born with an intact corpus callosum. However, a small number of children are born with a malformed or missing corpus callosum; a condition known as **callosal agenesis**. It has no known cause, and is thankfully very rare. It also seems that the absence of a corpus callosum often brings about other structural anomalies. For example, more pathways linking the front and back of each hemisphere are sometimes seen, and pathways between the hemispheres other than the corpus callosum are sometimes more fully developed.

Sadly, many acallosal children have multiple handicaps. However, some do not, and these children are of particular interest to psychologists because, in principle, they offer an opportunity to examine the role of the corpus callosum during development. If such individuals show the usual pattern of asymmetry, this would suggest that lateralisation is determined very early on in life and that the corpus callosum is not necessary for its development. If on the other hand, lateralisation is partly a developmental process that depends on the corpus callosum, we should find abnormalities of lateralisation in acallosal cases. It is also interesting to compare such individuals with split brain cases (Geffen and Butterworth 1992).

Research on 'acallosal' children indicates that they too have language skills lateralised usually to the left hemisphere, and spatial skills lateralised to the right. (These findings tend to support the first hypothesis that lateralisation is not gradually acquired during childhood.) However, people with callosal agenesis do seem to have certain difficulties with aspects of *both* language *and* spatial processing. In language tasks, there seem to be difficulties when the sound of the word is important. This becomes apparent in rhyming tasks, or when the subject is asked to generate words that sound alike, such as cart, heart, start and so on. Adding to this picture, acallosals often seem to have difficulties with spatial tasks such as jigsaws, copying drawings, puzzles, depth perception and so on. The reasons for these deficits are not known, but we should remember that it would be inaccurate to describe the brains of people with callosal agenesis as 'normal apart from missing the corpus callosum'.

Other psychological deficits probably relate to the general problem of inter-hemispheric transfer. Indeed, a strong hint about the role of the corpus callosum in cortical functioning comes from the observation that acallosal children and adults are very clumsy in tasks that require bi-manual dexterity (using both hands). Examples include playing an instrument, doing certain sports, or even tying shoelaces.

In certain respects, acallosal adults are rather like normal young children whose corpus callosum is immature. Its presence seems less involved in the process of shaping asymmetry than in promoting collaboration between the hemispheres; a point which we reconsider in due course.

Evaluation of research with acallosal individuals

In many cases of callosal agenesis other brain abnormalities are present as well. This makes it difficult for psychologists to identify with any confidence those behavioural disturbances which have resulted specifically from the absence of a corpus callosum. In cases where meaningful data has been collected, it seems that asymmetries occur regardless, suggesting that the corpus callosum is not necessary for lateralisation to develop. However, the general clumsiness and lack of two-handed co-ordination seen in acallosals remind us of the importance of inter-hemispheric communication (made possible by the corpus callosum) for normal behaviour.

Asymmetries in normal individuals

We can also study lateralisation in normal individuals with intact brains using a variety of procedures. One is the dichotic listening task as used by Kimura and colleagues. This procedure relies on the fact that most auditory input to the right ear is relayed to the opposite auditory cortex for detailed processing, and vice versa for the left ear. The idea is to present different strings of words simultaneously to both ears (via stereo headphones), and ask the respondent to report what is heard, or alternatively whether or not particular words are heard. Most research of this kind shows a small but consistent right ear advantage for linguistic material. This is thought to occur because words heard by the right ear are processed directly by the left (linguistic) hemisphere, whereas words heard by the left ear are initially processed by the right (non-verbal) hemisphere, before being relayed to the left hemisphere for semantic (i.e. meaning) analysis. It could be that this finding is related to greater sensitivity or acuity in the right ear generally. However, this cannot be so because the right ear advantage is reversed if the message is non-verbal (e.g. musical; Bartholomeus 1974).

The same general pattern of right field advantage for verbal material and left field advantage for non-verbal material appears to hold in the visual and tactile modalities too. For example, normal subjects can recognise words more quickly when they are presented briefly (using a tachistoscope or computer) to the right visual field, and faces more efficiently when presented to the left visual field.

Asymmetry can also be seen in relation to movement. Whilst most humans are right-handed, a motor skill performed with the right hand is more likely to be interfered with by a concurrent language task than the same skill performed by the left hand. You can test this in a very simple experiment. Ask a friend to balance a stick or pole using only the fingers of either the left or right hand. When they have mastered this task, ask them to shadow (i.e. repeat as soon as they hear it) a paragraph of text that you read out loud. The concurrent verbal task will usually affect right hand balance sooner than left hand balance. Try it out!

Which of the following statements is true or false and why?

a) a split brain subject can draw with his left hand an object flashed to the right hemisphere
b) a split brain subject cannot identify any words presented briefly to the left of a fixation point
c) a split brain subject has difficulty completing tasks which involve using both hands
d) split brain subjects frequently appear to contradict themselves
e) acallosal individuals probably make more use of other inter-hemispheric pathways to enable communication between the hemispheres
f) a split brain subject appears to be better at recognising faces presented briefly in the right visual field than the left.

Progress exercise

What is lateralised?

The evidence from brain-damaged, split brain, acallosal and normal individuals reviewed so far points to a division of labour along the lines of language: left hemisphere, spatial skills: right hemisphere, and this model has been the dominant one until quite recently. Yet a moment's thought suggests that if this were the entire story, our brains would be working in a very inefficient way! As we played with a jigsaw puzzle our left hemispheres could take a nap, and as we struggled with a crossword puzzle, our right hemispheres could do likewise.

An alternate explanation which has grown in popularity in recent years is that the two hemispheres process information in different ways (the 'processing styles' approach). According to this view the left hemisphere can be thought of as processing information in what has been described as an 'analytical-sequential' way, whereas the right hemisphere adopts a more 'holistic-parallel' mode of processing. Although these ideas sound complicated they really mean that the left hemisphere breaks tasks down into smaller elements which are dealt with one by one, whereas the right hemisphere tends to ignore the fine detail, paying more attention to the 'big picture'.

This model allows for the possibility that *both* hemispheres may be involved in linguistic or spatial tasks, but that they differ in the type of processing that is undertaken. For example, the right hemisphere is better at judging whether two facial photographs are of the same person. This is a holistic skill because face recognition involves putting together 'the face' from its individual elements. However, the left hemisphere is better at identifying individual facial features that may distinguish between two otherwise identical faces (an analytic skill, because it requires the 'whole' to be broken down into its constituent parts). Language is both sequential and analytical. (Sequential because word order is critical for meaning, and analytical since the meaning of language depends on analysis of the verbal message). It is thus dealt with mainly by the left hemisphere, whereas spatial skills including face recognition require holistic analysis and are thus dealt with by the right hemisphere.

The different processing styles of the two hemispheres were very clearly illustrated in a study by Sergent (1982). She developed a set of visual stimuli that were large capital letters, made up of small letters that were either the same as, or different to the capital letter. The stimuli were shown briefly via a tachistoscope to either the left or right visual fields of normal subjects. Their task was to indicate whether or not particular target letters were present. On some trials, subjects were directed to attend to the large capital letters, and at other times they were cued to attend to the small letters (that made up the big capitals). Sergent found that the left hemisphere (right visual field presentation) was better at detecting the small letters, and the right hemisphere (left visual field presentation) was better for the large letters. (See Chapter 8 for a review of the study carried out by Delis *et al.* (1986) which follows up Sergent's work, and Figure 4.5 for an example of the stimuli Sergent and Delis *et al.* used.)

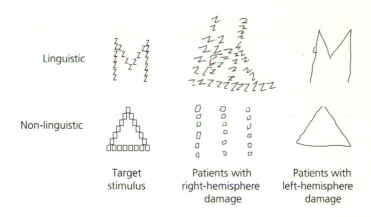

Linguistic

Non-linguistic

Target
stimulus

Patients with
right-hemisphere
damage

Patients with
left-hemisphere
damage

Figure 4.5 **Sergent's stimuli and the results of the study carried
out by Delis *et al.***

Source: Delis *et al.* (1986). Reprinted with permission from Elsevier
Science Ltd.

Notes: Patients who sustain damage to the right hemisphere can
correctly draw the local, or component, parts of the objects, as illustrated
by the correct drawing of the Zs and the rectangles. However, the overall
global form is incorrect; it is neither an *M* in the case of the linguistic
stimulus) nor a triangle (in the case of the non-linguistic stimulus). In
contrast, patients who sustain damage to the left hemisphere can
correctly draw the global form of the items but not the local, or component parts.

Evaluation of the 'processing styles' approach

These studies show us that rather than having a division of labour, the hemispheres may have complementary processing roles. The right hemisphere sees (so to speak) the forest, whilst the left hemisphere sees the trees. The right hemisphere processes information at a coarser level than the left which deals with information at a more detailed and local level. As an analytical and sequential skill language is dealt with predominantly (but not exclusively) by the left hemisphere. Spatial tasks, which usually involve integrative rather than analytic skills, are handled primarily by the right hemisphere.

This model of hemispheric specialisation, with its emphasis on processing style rather than psychological function, makes much better sense of the research data than the traditional model of left brain: language, right brain: spatial skills, and is becoming widely accepted by psychologists. However, in one sense it still doesn't entirely explain the 'seamless' nature of psychological functioning. People do not generally feel that they have two separate processors in their heads set to operate at different levels of analysis. On the contrary, we feel that we have one brain, and we also tend to respond serially. Remember that despite our otherwise remarkable psychological skills, humans actually have difficulty doing two different things at once. You will no doubt know the playground prank in which a child tries to pat his/her head and rub his/her stomach at the same time!

Inter-hemispheric transfer via the corpus callosum

Earlier we had a hint about how 'unity' may be achieved when we considered the effects of lesioning the corpus callosum. For example, Sergent (1990) showed that split brain subjects had difficulty in deciding whether (or not) pairs of photographs presented briefly and simultaneously to right and left visual fields were of the same or different people. Normal people, on the other hand, can often complete this sort of task without error, even when the photographs are taken from a variety of different angles and perspectives. The findings illustrate the importance of the corpus callosum in integrating the activity of the two hemispheres. Although other pathways exist connecting the two sides of the brain, it is the corpus callosum which enables the two hemispheres of the cortex to communicate with each other, and to relay information backwards and forwards almost instantaneously. ERP recording has shown that inter-hemispheric transfer takes no more than 20 milliseconds.

Developmental aspects

The human corpus callosum is made up almost entirely of myelinated axons and it develops throughout childhood (as more myelin is deposited), reaching full maturity only in adolescence. However, evidence of hemispheric specialisation is apparent even in very young children, and it is also apparent in the acallosal individuals we discussed earlier. These findings indicate that the corpus callosum is probably not critical in determining hemispheric specialisation; or even in its development.

Developmental studies on very young children suggest that lateralisation is essentially a feature of basic nervous system development, and probably under genetic control. For example, in babies only one week old, brain activity was greater on the left side in response to verbal nonsense stimuli ('pa' or 'ba') and greater on the right side in response to non-verbal auditory stimuli such as musical chords or bells (Best *et al.* 1982).

If this pattern of specialisation is apparent so early on, what happens if the normal developmental process is interrupted or disabled in some way? We can partly answer this question by considering what happens to children who are born with one malformed or very small hemisphere. Thankfully such instances are rare, but when they do occur, the preferred course of action is to remove the hemisphere altogether, to eliminate it as a source of potential epileptic activity in later life. In these children, whilst some language and spatial skills usually develop, those with only a left hemisphere outperform those with only a right hemisphere on linguistic tasks, whilst the opposite is found for spatial tasks (Dennis and Kohn 1975). However, it is important to note that such children are rarely as able at either sort of task as normal children, and this is equally true for children who have 'lost' a hemisphere due to an accident early in life.

In general, these data show that, in humans, hemispheric specialisation is determined very early on. However, when the normal pattern of development is not possible, the cortex is sufficiently adaptable ('plastic') to facilitate *some* transfer of function to the other hemisphere. In neuropsychology, 'plasticity' is a major research interest at the moment, and I review a study in this area by Mogilner *et al.* (1993) in Chapter 8. For the moment, we can say that the kind of 'plastic' changes I have just described in young children become less likely as the nervous system matures.

Individual differences in brain organisation

To conclude this chapter, we consider the extent to which the pattern of lateralisation described above varies between people. Two areas where this question seems particularly relevant (and controversial) are handedness and gender.

Handedness

From developmental studies it is clear that handedness is something you are born with rather than something you acquire with experience. Indeed, researchers using ultra-sound have reported that hand preference is actually apparent in unborn babies judging by their preference for sucking either left or right hand digits! About one-in-ten humans is left-handed according to Annett (1985), although degree of left- or right-handedness certainly varies. Left-handedness has, historically, been frowned on, and at one time, it was common practice for 'natural' left-handers to be forced to use their non-dominant right hands, both at school, and at home. Interestingly, as this practice has faded, the proportion of left-handers has increased, but only to the figure cited above.

For many years it was more or less assumed by psychologists that the organisation of the left-hander's brain was the mirror image of that of the right-hander. However, the advent of in-vivo imaging and use of the Wada test put paid to this myth. Results indicated that for right handers, the pattern of lateralisation described in this chapter was found in almost all individuals. For left-handers, a different result emerged. About 70% have the same arrangement as right-handers. Of the remainder, half (that is 15%) show the opposite pattern (reversed asymmetry) and half (the other 15%) show language and spatial skills both to be distributed in each hemisphere (bilateral distribution).

We might ask: 'Are there any psychological consequences of being left-handed?' Some psychologists have tried to answer this question by examining psychological function in right- and left-handed individuals who have incurred brain damage. One of the most comprehensive reviews of neurological cases was reported by Hardyck and Petrinovich (1977). They found that on average, left-handers with damage to the right-hemisphere were more likely to experience language problems than right-handers (14% versus 7%). The incidence of aphasia following left-sided damage was the same for right- and left-handers. Similarly, spatial functioning was more likely to be affected after right hemisphere damage in right-handers than in left-handers. These findings suggest that left-handers as a group may be less 'lateralised' than right-handers, in the sense that there may be less separation of psychological functions. Research on normal left-handers using tests of both dichotic listening and divided visual attention has also led to the suggestion that left-handers are less lateralised than right-handers.

However, are these results so surprising? Remember that some left-handers show left hemisphere dominance, some show right hemisphere dominance and some show mixed patterns. So as a group, we would *expect* to find that left-handers were less lateralised *on average* than right-handers! Perhaps the more interesting question would be to compare test performance between left-handers with left, right and mixed dominance patterns, but at present large scale studies of this type have yet to be undertaken.

Handedness and cognitive function

Despite these reassurances, left-handedness continues to be the subject of intrigue and speculation. For example, it has long been known that left-handedness is more common amongst mentally handicapped and reading-delayed individuals. Levy (1969) reported that left-handers have a small but consistent generalised non-verbal IQ deficit as measured by the WAIS: (left-handed readers might begin to feel especially indignant at this point!) Unfortunately, or perhaps fortunately, Levy's research findings have not been well-supported in follow-up studies, and where differences have been reported, they have usually been very small.

Sex differences

One of the most controversial areas of research has been the question of psychological differences between the sexes, and how these might be related to brain organisation. There are good reasons for thinking that there might be differences in brain organisation (or at least function) between the sexes: boys are known to be about twice as likely to be born with a range of CNS developmental disorders as girls. It has been estimated that at birth the general level of tissue development in boys is between 4 and 6 weeks behind that of girls. It is also well documented that disorders including autism, hyperactivity, stutter, aphasia and dyslexia are all four to six times more common in boys than girls. There are also consistent anatomical differences in brain structure which are found even in very young children.

One of the most comprehensive reviews of sex differences and behaviour was that of MacCoby and Jacklin (1974). Although their research also included measures related to social play and aggression, most interest was probably generated by their conclusion that girls tended to do better (more or less from the word go) at language related skills, and boys tended to do better at visuo-spatial skills. For example, if we consider the linguistic data, girls begin to talk earlier, they develop a greater vocabulary, and they learn to read earlier. These differences can be seen almost as soon as it is possible to measure them, and they increase through childhood and adolescence: Teenage girls, for example, have consistently higher scores for comprehension, fluency and translation. Boys, on the other hand, are better at tasks of visual tracking, aiming, maze learning, mental rotation, and map reading. We cannot rule out the possibility that some of these differences are acquired through experience, but their appearance so early in development suggests that they are, in part at least, a consequence of differential brain organisation.

These ideas have been taken up by many researchers including Kimura and her colleagues, and their research has helped to clarify some of the differences first described by MacCoby and Jacklin. As with the earlier debate about the functions of the left and right hemispheres, the rather simplistic conclusions drawn by early researchers (that boys are better at visuo-spatial skills and girls are better at linguistic skills) has been revised.

Take the skill of route learning as an example. In this visuo-spatial task, a subject has to learn an imaginary or real route from A to B on a map. Boys as young as 3 years old find this sort of task easier to do than girls (Kimura 1992). However, once learned, girls remember more landmarks along the route than boys! As with the earlier laterality research, this finding raises again the possibility that boys and girls employ different strategies to complete the task. Perhaps boys form an abstract plan of the relationship between points A and B, whereas girls negotiate the route via a series of landmarks. In support of this hypothesis Kimura (1992) has reported that girls are consistently better at the party game in which they are allowed to look around a room, blindfolded and then, when the blindfold is removed, asked to identify objects in the room that have been moved or taken away. Boys, on the other hand, having seen a particular room layout, are better at avoiding bumping into things when blindfolded.

The same pattern of findings emerges from the neurological literature. McGlone (1980) reported on a large number of case studies of people who had suffered damage to just one side of their brain. Left-sided damage was more likely to result in impaired language function in men than women. Right-sided damage was more likely to impair visuo-spatial function in men than women. There are two possible explanations of this finding. One is that language and spatial abilities are more bilaterally controlled (i.e. distributed in both hemispheres) in women than men; the other is that women tend to use verbally mediated strategies to solve *both* linguistic and visuo-spatial problems. At present it is not possible to say which of these is more likely, but the second explanation tallies well with Kimura's theory of strategy differences between the sexes.

Identify

   a) three structural differences
   b) three functional differences
   c) one difference related to handedness
   d) one difference related to sex

between the left and right hemispheres.

Review exercise

Summary

The research that I have reviewed in this chapter supports a model of hemispheric specialisation in humans. Whilst it would be an oversimplification to call the left hemisphere the language hemisphere and the right hemisphere the spatial (or non-language) hemisphere, it is easy to see why earlier researchers jumped to this conclusion. Research has been conducted on people with brain damage, with surgically lesioned or absent corpus callosa, and on normal people. This all points to a 'primary' responsibility in the left hemisphere for language. This does not mean that all language skills are, somehow, contained within this hemisphere. Rather that, on balance, this hemisphere 'has the final say' when it comes to language (no pun intended!). Whether this is because the left-hemisphere is pre-ordained for language, or because the left hemisphere is innately better at analytic and sequential processing (both of which language involves) is currently a matter of debate. Certainly, right hemisphere processing seems to be more holistic and integrative. Finally, we have seen that lateralisation can, to some extent, be modified by both handedness and sex differences.

Further reading

Banich, M. (1997) *Neuropsychology: The neural bases of mental function*, Boston, MA: Houghton-Mifflin, chapter 3. A more academic account of lateralisation research covering the neurological and split brain material, psychological research with 'normals', and research on handedness and sex differences.

Springer, S.P. and Deutsch, G. (1993) *Left Brain, Right Brain*, Freeman & Co: New York. The entire book is a delight. Written in very down-to-earth language, and littered with illustrations from the authors' own clinical research, the division of labour between the hemispheres is reviewed from all angles.

5

Sensory and motor function

Introduction

When psychologists talk about sensory and motor function they really mean input to and output from the nervous system. For example, the traffic light changes to red (sensory input), and you press the brake pedal (motor output). As you now know, the mammalian brain has large specialised areas dedicated to receiving and interpreting sensory input (separately for each modality), and making appropriate motor responses. These so-called sensory and motor regions of the cortex are not the only parts of the brain concerned with sensation and movement; several other cortical areas, and some sub-cortical structures are also involved. However, they have direct responsibilities, and are known as the **primary sensory cortex** and **primary motor cortex** respectively. We shall consider some of these areas, and their connections to the rest of the nervous system in this chapter.

However, we start with a reminder that plenty of sensory input and quite a lot of motor output never involves the conscious brain at all, being handled at a lower level of processing in the spinal cord. Actually, in non-primates, this is a common pattern: stories about headless chickens running around the farmyard are, apparently, true!

Reflexes

In relation to the evolutionary scale, the behaviour of the higher mammals, and especially primates, depends more and more on brain power, and comparatively less on the spinal cord and peripheral nervous system. Yet even in humans the brain's monopoly is incomplete, and we regularly *sense* and *respond* without it: a good example of this would be one of the simple reflex responses, of which the best known is probably the knee jerk reflex. Tapping the tendon just below the knee causes a reflex 'jerking up' of the lower leg. Here, the sensory input is the tap, and the response is the twitch … but what, exactly, is happening? Nature did not design this system just to enable your doctor to check your reflexes, but I will delay revealing its purpose until I have explained how it works. For the moment think of it as a fairly primitive (and simple) form of sensory–motor co-ordination. The knee jerk reflex works like this.

- When the tendon is tapped, it is stretched.
- The tendon stretch causes special sensory receptors (on the surface of the tendon) to stretch too. As a result, they generate nerve impulses (action potentials) which travel towards the spinal cord signalling 'stretch'.
- In the simplest case, in the spinal cord, there is a synapse between the sensory neuron (carrying 'stretch' information), and a motor neuron which connects to the thigh muscle. Stimulation from the sensory neuron causes the motor neuron to produce its own nerve impulses.
- When these nerve impulses get to the end of the motor neuron, there is a synapse with the thigh muscle, and synaptic transmission causes it to contract.
- The muscle contraction causes the lower leg to kick up or twitch!

Now that I have explained the mechanism, have you any ideas about its probable function? The most likely answer is that this type of reflex contributes to balance and posture by bringing about rapid readjustments of muscle tension following unexpected extension or stretching. Imagine walking along a very bumpy path without this 'self-correcting' mechanism. You would be likely to trip up every time you came across a bump or a pothole!

As I mentioned earlier, although reflexes like the knee jerk do not involve the brain, they are a useful model to help us understand the basic layout of sensory and motor functions. There is sensory input, some kind of central processing (a single synapse in the spinal cord in this case) and a motor response. However, we should remember that humans can sense without necessarily making overt (observable) responses. We can also respond in the absence of sensory input, as for example, in putting some plan or intention into effect. Therefore, we should consider the input and output sides separately, although, as you will see, they often work in collaboration, and share many common features.

With this model in mind, it's now time to consider the layout of sensory and motor systems in higher mammals. Although humans are said to have at least five senses, in this chapter I have chosen to focus on the somatosensory system, which is concerned with touch and other related sensory input. (In Chapter 7, I review the visual pathways too.)

The somatosensory system

This is known as a poly-modal system, meaning it combines a variety of sensory inputs. Firstly, it provides us with a constantly updated picture of tactile (touch, pressure, vibration) input on the body surface (this is called *exteroceptive* information, because it originates outside the body). Secondly, it deals with information about the relative position of body parts, and the position of the body in space (so-called *interoceptive* information, from within the body). Thirdly, for good measure, it processes information about heat and cold, and pain too.

As with any sensory system, sensory input must first be converted into nerve impulses or action potentials. This process, called **transduction**, is performed by receptors that are located in skin, joints, or as we have seen, on muscles or tendons. In mammals there are at least 20 different types of receptors to deal with information about touch, temperature, stretch, pain and so on. Their job is to generate action potentials when stimulated. Receptors tend to be individually 'tuned' to be most active to different intensities of stimulation. For example some of the touch receptors are particularly sensitive to light touch, others to tickle, and still others to vibration or pressure.

Somatosensory pathways

Information (in the form of patterns or volleys of action potentials), has to be relayed from the receptors to the central nervous system. (How else would the brain get to know about somatosensory stimulation?) In this sensory system, the receptors mentioned earlier are modified neurons, and their axons run from the point of stimulation towards the spinal cord. Many of these axons are myelinated, which improves the speed of conduction of action potentials dramatically.

On entering the spinal cord, some sensory neurons continue uninterrupted up to the brain along pathways known as **dorsal columns** (because they are at the back of the cord). In other cases, they synapse as they enter the spinal cord onto spinal neurons, which then convey the information along their axons to the brain rather like a relay race. This second set of pathways are known as the **spino-thalamic tracts**. The pathways can be distinguished in terms of the information they convey too. The former carries precise 'fine grained' localised information, the latter carries coarser, less precisely localised information to do with pain and temperature. Most somatosensory input crosses on its way to the brain from one side of the body to the other, giving rise to what psychologists call **contralateral control**. Information from the left side of the body finds its way to the right thalamus, cortex and so on.

The route from receptor to cortex has involved relays of two or three neurons (and one or two synapses), yet the time it takes to convey information along the pathways is typically measured in fractions of a second. However, in some cases, speed of conduction is significantly slower. Pain information for example, which is carried along narrow unmyelinated neurons, may take 1 or 2 seconds to register in the brain. This explains why there is sometimes a brief delay between incurring injury (say a burn to the skin) and feeling pain.

Somatosensory cortex

Like other sensory systems the somatosensory cortex has a primary area for stimulus registration, and other areas (known as secondary and tertiary areas) for sensory integration and recognition. In humans, the primary area occupies a strip of cortex that runs approximately from ear to ear across the top of the brain. Strictly speaking, it is the most anterior (forward) gyrus (bump) of the parietal lobe (see Figure 5.1a).

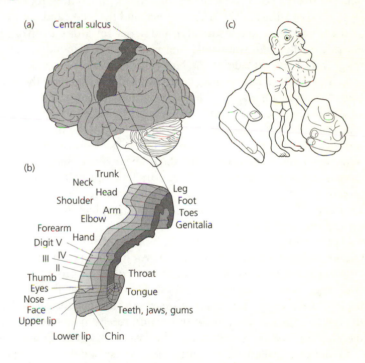

Figure 5.1 Topographic representation in the somatosensory cortex

Source: Rosenzweig *et al.* (1996: 268). Reprinted with permission from Sinauer Associates, Sunderland, MA.

Notes:
(a) The somatosensory strip.
(b) Topographic representation.
(c) A homunculus.

A truly remarkable feature of this band of cortex is that the entire body is mapped, or '**topographically represented**' along its length. To illustrate this, imagine you could record the activity of neurons in this band starting in the region of cortex located roughly behind the left ear. You would find that these neurons would only become active if there was stimulation to the right side of the tongue or jaw. A little further up, you would find neurons that were activated only to stimulation of the right cheek and forehead. Still further up, you would find neurons that respond to tactile stimulation of different parts of the right hand (with each part of each finger, and the palm, and the back of the hand represented separately), and so on. Towards the top of the left side of the brain you would find neurons that respond to tactile input from the right side of the body, the right leg, right ankle and foot. The identical mirror image pattern would be found on the right side of the somatosensory cortex. (If you think about it, it is difficult to see how else the system could operate, without losing 'topographic representation', but this does not diminish one's sense of wonder at the cortical mapping that occurs!) As methods of investigation have improved, it has become clear that the primary somatosensory cortex comprises not one but at least three parallel strips of neurons, each receiving distinct combinations of somatosensory input, whilst retaining the general pattern of topographic representation mentioned above (see Figure 5.1b).

The topographic representation is, however, distorted. Body areas that are more sensitive, such as the hands or lips, have proportionately very much larger areas of somatosensory cortex to project to than body regions that are less sensitive, such as the upper limbs or the back of the head. In fact, so far as we can tell for humans, about half the total number of neurons in this region receive input from either the face or hands. To illustrate this, early researchers drew or modelled so-called homunculi (little men) whose bodies were proportionate to the area of cortex sensitive to the various body regions (see Figure 5.1c). Interestingly, the same relationship (of sensitivity and dedicated cortex) is observed in other species. Mice for example, have disproportionately large regions of somatosensory cortex dedicated to snout and whiskers; cats have relatively large regions dedicated to tactile input from whiskers, paws and tail!

Secondary and tertiary somatosensory cortex

The primary somatosensory cortex is the initial point of processing of tactile input, and damage to it leads to reduced sensitivity for the particular body region which is connected to it. However, actual identification of objects by touch depends on other regions of cortex. The primary somatosensory cortex projects (sends outputs) to a secondary area whose role is to integrate input from the separate primary cortical strips, but now from both sides (i.e. bilaterally). Both of these areas project to other areas (the tertiary areas) of the parietal lobes behind (posterior to) the primary somatosensory strip.

We can get an idea of the sort of processing which takes place in the secondary and tertiary regions by considering the effects of localised damage here. As a general rule damage to more posterior regions affects higher order perceptual functioning, whilst leaving basic sensitivity unimpaired. Parietal damage often leads to one of the so-called **agnosias**: a curious and perplexing cluster of disorders which are described in more detail in Chapter 7. To give just one example here, damage to tertiary regions can lead to a condition I mentioned earlier known as astereognosis. In this disorder, blindfolded subjects can describe accurately the main physical features of objects that they feel, but cannot match them with other similar objects, or identify them by name.

Evaluation of research into the somatosensory system

Sensory input from all over the body is relayed via the spinal cord into the brain and eventually to the primary somatosensory strip. Here we find assemblies of neurons waiting (so to speak) for input from just one particular body region. Research has shown that the strip maps out the entire body contralaterally and upside down. We refer to this pattern of mapping as topographic representation, and evidence indicates that the pattern is very consistent from one person to the next. From here secondary and tertiary regions in the parietal lobe process the sensory input further, to enable perception and integration with other sensory modalities. Despite all that I have said so far in this chapter, recent research by psychologists has shown that under some circumstances (say after peripheral nerve damage) the primary somatosensory strip can rewire itself to some extent. I describe one such study by Mogilner *et al.* in Chapter 8.

Draw diagrams and/or figures to illustrate the function(s) of each of the following:

a) a simple reflex
b) receptors in the somatosensory system
c) the dorsal columns
d) the spino-thalamic tracts
e) topographic representation

Motor control

There is no getting away from the fact that brain control of movement is phenomenally complex. It has to be in order for individuals to engage in behaviours requiring precise muscle co-ordination. Think for a moment of the skill of the trained acrobat, or the dexterity of the concert pianist. But even mere mortals such as you and I can perform amazing motor feats. For example, try reciting aloud the alphabet as quickly as you can: you will probably be able to do it in about three seconds, or about one letter every 150 milliseconds. For each letter the mouth and vocal chords (muscles) have to be moved the correct distance in the right order and at the right time to articulate the required sounds. At the very least, this task requires understanding, intention, planning, and sequential co-ordination. Phenomenal!

Movement occurs when muscles contract. As we saw with the knee jerk reflex, this happens when motor neurons convey action potentials from the spinal cord to muscles. Working backwards, we might ask what influences the motor neurons ... ? A simple answer would be 'the brain', but as usual, the true picture is more complicated. First, there are not one but several pathways from different parts of the brain to the spinal cord where the cell bodies of motor neurons are located. Second, in the brain itself, there are several regions that are involved in the control movement: the frontal lobes of the cortex, the sub-cortical structures of the basal ganglia, and the cerebellum. Finally, there is good evidence that yet other brain regions such as the parietal lobes (usually associated with perceptual functions), may also be important in certain kinds of motor function.

The cerebral cortex and movement

Neurons in the cortex are not connected directly to muscles, but it has been known since the pioneering work of Fritsch and Hitzig (1870) that electrical stimulation of a region of cortex known as the primary motor strip can lead directly to movement. This strip is a band of tissue located immediately forward of the primary somatosensory cortex on the other side of the central sulcus. (Anatomically, it is the rear-most gyrus of the frontal lobes). Here we would find clusters of so-called pyramidal neurons whose axons descend within the brain to the medulla (mentioned in Chapter 2) and into the spinal cord, where they synapse with motor neurons. It is the motor neurons whose axons go to muscles.

Like the somatosensory cortex, the primary motor cortex is highly topographically organised. All regions of the body are represented, and there is almost exclusive contralateral control; the right motor cortex controls muscles in the left side of the body, and vice versa. Again, as with the somatosensory cortex, the relationship between cortical 'space' in the primary motor cortex and body region is not proportionate. Rather, there is over-representation of body regions capable of fine motor control, such as the hands and fingers, and the mouth area of the face.

With more precise instrumentation (basically, finer electrodes), researchers have discovered that the primary motor strip actually comprises not one but several parallel bands of topographically mapped pyramidal neurons (up to nine have been reported). Also, it seems that muscles actually require a pattern of activity in several adjacent cortical cells in order to bring about movement. This explains why damage to one or a few pyramidal cells weakens, but rarely eliminates entirely, movement in the corresponding body region.

In contrast, widespread damage to this region of cortex *does* bring about loss of muscle function and paralysis. In cases where accident or stroke has damaged the entire left or right primary motor cortex, the result is opposite side **hemiplegia** which usually involves lasting impairments.

Initiating movement

Having established the link between the primary motor cortex and muscles, we now need to consider how a person 'initiates' a movement. The answer to this question is only now emerging, and we know that other brain regions, in addition to the cortex are involved (see below). However, within the cortex the control of movement seems to be organised 'hierarchically' by different parts of the frontal lobes. As we mentioned in Chapter 2, in higher mammals the frontal lobes make up a significant proportion of total brain tissue (about 30% in humans). Given their size, we should expect to find functionally distinct regions in addition to the primary motor strip, and this turns out to be the case.

The hierarchy works like this. As we have already seen, pyramidal cells in the primary motor cortex control muscle contractions via their connections with motor neurons in the spinal cord. But these pyramidal cells are in turn partly controlled by neurons in the region of frontal lobe just forward of the primary motor cortex. This area is actually divided into two. There is the more medial **supplementary motor area or SMA** (towards the top of the brain) and the more lateral **pre-motor cortex** (towards the sides). Cells in each region influence the pyramidal cells in the primary cortex, when a particular movement is carried out. In other words, SMA and pre-motor cortex neurons control hierarchically the activity of individual pyramidal cells. (See Figure 5.2.)

So what controls the SMA and pre-motor cortex cells? The answer, again in part, is the area of frontal lobe *in front of them*. This area is known as the **pre-frontal area**, and it becomes active when an individual begins to plan a movement.

I can illustrate this hierarchical arrangement if we consider a very simple act such as drinking a glass of water.

- Initially, we may feel thirsty, and wish to quench our thirst. This motivational state is represented in the pre-frontal areas as a *plan* or *intention* to drink.
- The act of raising a glass, tipping and swallowing (called *a motor pattern*) is co-ordinated by the SMA and/or the pre-motor cortex. Incidentally, these areas control bilaterally. After all, you could pick up the glass with either hand.

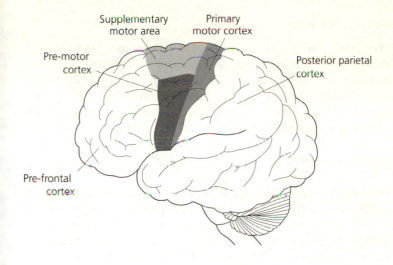

Figure 5.2   **Motor areas of the human cerebral cortex**

•   The SMA and pre-motor cortex control the pyramidal cells in the co-ordination of individual muscles as the glass is raised and the drink consumed.

Thus, there are three levels in the hierarchy; the plan, the motor pattern and the movement of individual muscles.

Empirical support for the hierarchical model

Although this organisational hierarchy has been speculated about for many years, the use of in-vivo imaging procedures such as SPECT and rCBF (discussed in Chapter 3) has confirmed it. Roland (1993) reported that when a subject was asked to complete a simple repetitive movement such as wiggling a finger, only the contralateral primary motor cortex shows increased activity. However, if a more complex sequence such as touching the ends of each finger with the thumb is required, both the SMA and the pre-frontal cortex show increased activity as well as the primary motor cortex. Even asking the subject to imagine the complex sequence causes increased activation in the SMA and pre-frontal regions.

Sub-cortical structures and movement

Damage to several non-cortical structures can also affect movement, so scientists have inferred that these must also contribute in some way to movement co-ordination. The structures in question are the various components of the basal ganglia, and the cerebellum. They cannot be considered in isolation however, because each has numerous connections with the cortex and spinal cord. (Since this book is primarily about the cortex, our consideration of these non-cortical components will be brief).

The basal ganglia   These are a group of sub-cortical structures (the names are not important, but check in Chapter 2 if you want to know) which connect with each other in a series of loops. The main input to the basal ganglia is from the frontal lobes (especially the SMA) and the main output is back to the frontal lobes, with a smaller output direct to the spinal cord. From clinical observations of people with Parkinson's disease, various other neurological disorders, and experimental studies with animals, it would seem that the basal ganglia operate like a volume control mechanism for the motor regions of the frontal lobes.

We have already seen that plans for movement originate in the prefrontal cortex and SMA. Clearly, each of us must, as adults, have hundreds if not thousands of plans stored away here (a plan for waving, a plan for scratching one's head and so on). The principal role of the basal ganglia seems to be to decide whether or not a particular plan should be put into effect. So, if the basal ganglia are overactive, as is the case in early stage Huntington's disease, unwanted excessive movements intrude, or become superimposed, on normal movements. This gives rise to the symptoms of unusual exaggerated trunk, limb, and facial movements. On the other hand, if the basal ganglia are underactive, as is the case in Parkinson's disease, planned actions fail to be put into effect, leading to the familiar features of the disease; slow or absent movements (including speech), rigidity, lack of facial expression and so on.

The cerebellum   This is one of the least well understood areas of the brain but we do know that damage to its various regions affects movement in different ways. Damage to the central region (known as the vermis) affects balance and posture. Damage to the more lateral regions affects movement of limbs, especially for tasks which require the co-ordinated movement of a limb (or limbs) over a period of time, such as typing or playing the guitar. Usually the movement can be completed, but instead of being smooth and well-rehearsed, it is jerky, tentative and often inaccurate. A classic test of cerebellar functioning is to ask a person to touch their nose with a finger whilst blindfolded. Try it; and as you are doing it imagine the co-ordination that is required of muscle movements (in time) as the finger approaches the nose! People with cerebellar damage can complete this test but it seems to be a struggle, and sometimes results in a sore eye! In general terms, people with this type of brain damage are clumsy and unco-ordinated, and they find it difficult to learn new motor skills.

Evaluation of motor systems in the mammalian brain

Earlier I said that separation of *cortical* and *sub-cortical* systems was to some extent artificial and now perhaps you can see why: both the basal ganglia and the lateral regions of the cerebellum receive inputs from and return outputs to the cortex. Roland has suggested that both sets of structures have similar but complementary roles. The basal ganglia interact with the SMA to enable (or inhibit) *internally* generated movement plans. The cerebellum interacts with the pre-motor region to regulate actions related to *external* stimuli or events. So the novice tennis player will rely mainly on the second set of connections to return serve, hoping to make contact with the ball (the external stimulus), and hit it anywhere in their opponent's court. The experienced player, on the other hand, will use both systems. The cere-bellar–cortical connections will control contact with the ball, and the basal ganglia–cortical connections will allow him/her (via internally generated intentions) to place his/her shot deliberately, to maximum advantage.

Review exercise

Write paragraphs of no more than 150 words comparing and contrasting each of the following pairs:

  a) the cortical and sub-cortical motor systems
  b) the roles of the pre-motor and pre-frontal cortex in movement
  c) the vermis and lateral cerebellum
  d) the primary motor and primary sensory strips

Summary

In this chapter, I have described some of the important features of the brain's role in sensation and movement. The somatosensory system combines different exteroceptive and interoceptive sensory input to provide a comprehensive picture of touch, the relative position of body parts, temperature and pain. Initial cortical processing takes place in the primary somatosensory strip which is topographically organised. Further (higher order) perceptual processing takes place in more posterior parts of the parietal lobe, and damage to these regions impairs perception of objects by touch.

The brain's control of movement is complex, involving a hierarchy of control centres within the frontal lobe. Other sub-cortical structures/systems including the cerebellum and basal ganglia contribute to the process through their connections with the frontal lobes. However, the complexity should not surprise us. After all, humans are not automatons capable only of producing set responses to particular stimuli. One factor that sets us apart from other animals is our ability to behave adaptively; to acquire new skills throughout our lives. The study of behaviour is, of course, really the study of movement, and our ability to learn new skills, and retain old ones (you never forget how to ride a bike) depends on the integrity and interconnections of the structures I have introduced in this chapter.

Further reading

Gazzaniga, M.S., Ivry, R.B. and Mangun, G.R. (1998) *Cognitive Neuroscience: The biology of the mind*, London: Norton, chapter 10. Motor control, comprehensively reviewed, with many illustrations of the effects of damage to different components of the system.

Kalat, J.W. (1998) *Biological Psychology*, 6th edn, Pacific Grove: Brooks/Cole, chapters 7 and 8. Superbly illustrated comprehensive reviews of how the mammalian brain (and the rest of the nervous system) deals with sensory input and co-ordinates motor output.

Language and the brain

Introduction

Of all psychological attributes, language is surely the one that sets humans apart. Other animals may use gestures and sounds to communicate, but the sheer complexity and sophistication of human language suggests to psychologists that extensive regions of the brain must be dedicated to dealing with it. Two factors have led researchers to conclude that humans are genetically predisposed to acquire language. One is the appearance of certain universal features, such as a basic grammatical form. A second is the ease with which language is acquired under the most adverse of circumstances (e.g. acquisition in deaf mute people).

Although it is not known for certain when language first appeared in the evolutionary sense, best estimates suggest that humans have used spoken language for at least 60,000 years. Written language is, of course, a much more recent phenomenon, and it is interesting to note that the brain regions which are involved in reading and writing are to some extent distinct from those involved in aural (spoken) language.

You may recall from Chapter 1 that interest in language dates back to the earliest attempts by researchers to study the brain in a systematic scientific way, with the work of Dax, Broca and Wernicke last century. In the meantime, interest in all aspects of language has intensified, to the point where its psychological study (**psycholinguistics**) is recognised as a discipline in its own right.

The history of the study of language mirrors that of the study of brain-behaviour relations in general. Early researchers tended to take a '*neurological approach*', relying on detailed 'case study' of a small number of individuals with brain damage of some sort, although it is now clear that the extent of damage was often uncertain. Broca, for example, based his ideas on research on only nine aphasic individuals, and his most famous patient 'Tan' is known to have had extensive damage to brain regions well outside the area we now call Broca's area. (See Figure 6.1.)

The development of new research techniques such as the Wada test, and more recently, in-vivo imaging procedures, has enabled

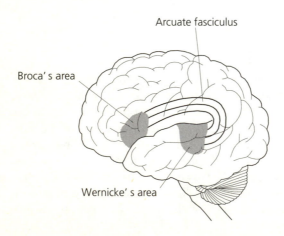

Figure 6.1   **Some important language areas**

researchers to examine language function in normal individuals. Perhaps predictably, this research has led to certain revisions to earlier ideas about how the brain deals with language. (As usual, the more closely one looks, the more complicated things appear!) However, despite the complexities, it is reassuring to note that research findings from several different perspectives are now producing converging results.

I start this chapter with a review of the classic neurological approach to language and a brief description of two of the best characterised forms of aphasia. Aphasia, you may recall, means impaired or lost language function. It is most commonly seen following brain damage or disease: for example, after diseases that affect supply of blood to the brain, such as a blood clot or haemorrhage (40% of stroke victims have some form of aphasia). It may result from disorders such as Alzheimer's disease, or it may occur following head injury (for example, after a road traffic accident).

In recent years there has been a move away from the strictly neurological approach which emphasises the organisation of the brain (for language). Instead, researchers have begun to examine the organisation of language (in the brain), and the specific language processes which may be lost after brain damage. I summarise the main areas of interest in psycholinguistics later in the chapter.

In-vivo imaging research into language is also introduced. This research has tended to support early 'classic' ideas of language in the brain; namely that language is mediated by a series of interconnected cortical regions in the left hemisphere. At the same time, in-vivo findings have shown that additional brain areas (some in the right hemisphere) are also involved. Firstly however, we revisit the classic neurology literature and clarify the nature of the best characterised aphasic conditions.

Broca's aphasia

Broca's aphasia is probably the best-documented language disorder. As with most neurological conditions, impairment is a matter of degree, but the main feature is a marked difficulty in producing coherent speech. (For this reason, some textbooks call Broca's aphasia 'expressive' or 'non-fluent' aphasia.) Broca's patient 'Tan' could, if you remember, only utter the one word, but most of Broca's aphasics can speak. However, they seem to have problems in finding the words they want to use, and prepositions, conjunctions (words like in, and, but, and so on) and other relational words are often omitted. As a result, speech is slow, deliberate, and has only a very simple grammatical structure. Indeed, the term 'telegraphic speech' has often been used as a short-hand description for Broca's aphasia speech. ('Need drink, pour … glass … thirsty'.)

Interestingly, Broca's aphasics can often use well-practised expressions without obvious difficulty ('Shall we have a cuppa?'). They may also be able to sing a well-known song faultlessly. Reading aloud will usually not be impaired. These exceptions show us that the problem is not related to 'the mechanics' of moving the muscles that are concerned with speech, and to underline this point, Broca's aphasics have similar 'agrammatical' problems when trying to write. (See Box 6.1.)

The alternative name of 'expressive' aphasia is a reminder that the most obvious features of this condition relate to difficulties in language production. However, some Broca's aphasics also have problems with comprehension although this is only apparent when the meaning of a sentence depends critically on its grammatical structure. (For example, this sentence may cause problems: 'The girl, who the boy was watching, was talking with friends'. The test is to see if the respondent knows who was watching whom.) A further feature of Broca's aphasia is that the affected individual is usually well aware of their own difficulties, and almost always has some 'insight' into their condition.

We use the term 'Broca's area' to describe the region of cortex on the left side that Broca associated with this form of aphasia. The region in question is in the frontal lobe, forward from the primary motor cortex, towards the side, roughly in front of and slightly above the left ear. However, recent research indicates that Broca's aphasia probably depends on more extensive damage than Broca originally thought. Adjacent cortical regions, or areas of cortex normally hidden from view in the sulci (folds) under the surface have also been implicated (one candidate area is the insular region). Incidentally, deaf people with brain damage in this region have trouble producing sign language.

Box 6.1: Broca's aphasia

THERAPIST: Tell me about your recent holiday.

PATIENT: ...Well ... Well now ... (*long pause*). We ... err ... I ... holiday ... you know ...

THERAPIST: What happened?

PATIENT: ...Oh, we ... err ... holiday ... you know ... seaside ...

THERAPIST: Tell me some more.

PATIENT: Beautiful weather ... (*shows off suntan on arm*).

THERAPIST: Where did you get that?

PATIENT: (*bursts into song*) Oh, I do like to be beside the seaside ... Oh I do like to be beside the sea ... (*broad grin*).

THERAPIST: Did you go with your sister?

PATIENT: Sister ... yes ... sister. To ... On holi ... holiday ... In a cara ... cara ... cara-thingy ... caravan! That's it! A cara ... caravan.

THERAPIST: Did you take her, or did she take you?

PATIENT: Hey! You're ... you're ... trying to catch ... catch me out ...! (*grins broadly again*).

THERAPIST: I just wondered who made the arrangements?

PATIENT: We...we...you know, we go here ... every ... each ... you know ... year. Same place, same time, same girl (*laughs at own joke*).

Wernicke's aphasia

In 1874, Wernicke described a patient with damage to a region of brain further back than the area linked with Broca's aphasia, in the upper part of the left temporal lobe (the superior temporal gyrus, a little above and behind the ear) (see Figure 6.1). This patient had difficulty in understanding speech but could speak fluently. Unfortunately, what he said usually did not make much sense. This form of aphasia differed fundamentally from that described by Broca. The main problems for Wernicke's patient were related to comprehension and meaningful output. The fluent but nonsensical speech of someone with Wernicke's aphasia (as it became known) is all the harder to understand because of two further characteristic features.

One is the patient's use of non-words or made-up words (known as *neologisms*). A second is the absence of 'insight': they may talk nonsense without realising it, yet they are unaware that other people cannot understand them! (See Box 6.2.)

Box 6.2: Wernicke's aphasia

THERAPIST: What's this for? (*shows patient a hammer*)

PATIENT: Oh Boy! That's a ... that's a thingy for ... thing for ...

THERAPIST: Yes, but what is it?

PATIENT: It? I dunno ... Umm ... It's a nisby thing though! (*chuckles to himself*)

THERAPIST: How about this? (*shows patient a nail*)

PATIENT: That? Well, see you have those all over the place ... In the doors, on the floors ... everywhere's got 'em ...

THERAPIST: What is it?

PATIENT: Mmm...See, I don't really get there much see, so ... you know, it's kind of hard for me to spray ...

THERAPIST: (*hands patient the nail*) Do you recognise it now?

PATIENT: Let's see now ... its sort of sharp, and long, and cold in the wintertime don't you think ...? (*pretends to shiver*).

THERAPIST: Do you use this (*points to the hammer again*) with that? (*points to the nail*).

PATIENT: Mmm. That's a good one! (*laughs again*) Let's see now, a screw and a nail eh? Maybe in a toolboss ... Yes! That's it; they all go in the toolboss in the back of the shed you see. In the garden ... the shed, in the toolboss.

Wernicke thought that the underlying deficit in this condition was a problem in linking sound images to meaning. He presented neuroanatomical support for this idea when he performed a post-mortem on one of his patients. Damage was most marked in the left temporal regions immediately behind the area of primary auditory cortex. This area, also known as **Heschl's gyrus**, receives massive inputs from the ears, and is where speech sounds undergo initial analysis. Damage to the areas of cortex just behind Heschl's gyrus is usually found in cases of Wernicke's aphasia.

Wernicke thought that the region of brain he had identified would be connected anatomically to the brain region implicated in Broca's aphasia. Moreover, damage to the pathway between the two areas alone might give rise to another form of aphasia. In this case, there would be a disconnection between the area for speech sounds (Wernicke's area), and the area for speech output (Broca's area), although the two areas themselves need not be damaged! The pathway in question is called the **arcuate fasciculus**. Can you guess what aphasic condition may result from damage to it? The answer is a form of aphasia known as 'conduction aphasia', in which both comprehension and speech production are preserved, but the ability to repeat words is lost!

Read the interviews in Boxes 6.1 and 6.2 again. Find one example of each of the following, and comment on it.

a) a neologism
b) telegraphic speech
c) nonsensical speech
d) evidence of insight
e) evidence of lack of insight

Progress exercise

Connectionist models of language

Broca's and Wernicke's work generated considerable interest amongst fellow researchers. In 1885, Lichtheim proposed what has come to be known as his *connectionist model of language* to explain the various forms of aphasia (seven in all) that had, by then, been described. Incidentally, the term 'connectionist' is similar to the term 'distributed control' which I introduced in Chapter 1. It implies that different brain centres are interconnected, and that impaired language function may result either from damage to one of the centres or to the pathways between centres.

In Lichtheim's model, Broca's and Wernicke's areas formed two points of a triangle. The third point represented a 'concept' centre

where auditory comprehension occurred. Each point was interconnected, so that damage, either to one of the centres (points), or to any
of the pathways connecting them would induce some form of
aphasia. Lichtheim's model explained many of the peculiarities of
different forms of aphasia, and became the dominant model of how
the brain manages language comprehension and production for the
next one hundred years. (See Figure 6.2.) In the 1960s it received
further support following work by the psychologist Geschwind (e.g.
Geschwind 1967).

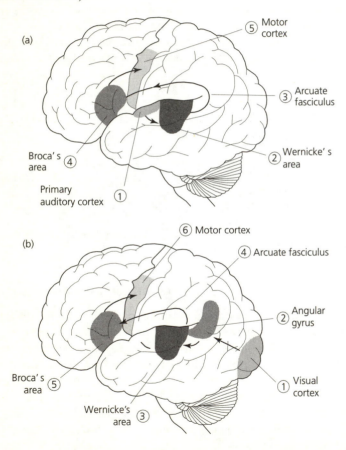

Figure 6.2 **The connectionist model for (a) speaking a heard word
and (b) speaking a written word**

The exact location of the concept centre in Lichtheim's description, was unclear. Geschwind proposed that in fact, there were two cortical concept centres, concerned with motor and sensory concepts respectively; the former located in the frontal lobes, and the latter in the left parietal lobe, closely linked to (but separate from) Wernicke's area. Damage to these regions, or the connections between them and the other centres readily explained the features of two further rare aphasic conditions now known respectively as motor and sensory **trans-cortical aphasia**. The motor form is like Broca's aphasia, but in addition, there is an absence of spontaneous speech. Another feature is a marked tendency to repeat things aloud, which sometimes appears almost compulsive and is called '*echolalia*'. In the sensory form, difficulty with comprehension resembles that seen in Wernicke's aphasia. However, repetition is intact. Indeed, as with the motor form, echolalia may even be prominent.

To complete the picture, extensive damage to multiple parts of Lichtheim's system would lead to **global aphasia**; a profound form of impairment affecting both comprehension and production of language.

Although Geschwind's work led to renewed interest in the connectionist model of language, other research findings seemed not to fit particularly well with it. For example, some individuals were found who seemed to have damage to Wernicke's area but who did not show general impairments in comprehension. (This finding parallels that related to concerns about the anatomical basis of Broca's aphasia reviewed earlier.) Other Wernicke's patients showed substantial recovery over time. Some made a complete recovery from Wernicke's aphasia, but were left with a condition known as **pure word deafness**. In this condition, people can hear speech, but they cannot understand it. Recent anatomical and imaging research has shown that pure word deafness probably results from damage either to Wernicke's area itself, or to the pathway connecting Hechl's gyrus to it. Wernicke's aphasia, on the other hand, depends on damage to more extensive cortical regions where the temporal and parietal lobes converge, and to the white matter underlying Wernicke's area (Dronkers 1996).

Evaluation of the neurological approach to language

The study of language impairment in people with brain damage has provided a wealth of information about the role(s) of left-sided cortical regions involved in mediating language. The types of aphasia identified over 100 years ago are still seen today, and careful case study has thrown up several other forms of language disorder which can be related to lesions/damage to other components of the brain's language system. On the other hand, human brain damage is, inevitably, highly variable. Recent research has led psychologists to conclude that the forms of aphasia identified by Broca and Wernicke probably depend on more extensive damage to either frontal or posterior regions than was initially thought. Also, it appears that several other 'centres' (and interconnecting pathways) in addition to Broca's and Wernicke's areas and the arcuate fasciculus are involved. These contribute to a distributed control network that is responsible for the full range of language skills. Finally, it is worth mentioning again that there is potential danger in relying on the study of damaged brains to form an understanding of normal brain function.

The psycholinguistic approach

Psycholinguistics is, primarily, the study of the structure of language in normal individuals, rather than the study of language impairments of neurological patients. As the discipline grew, researchers developed theories about the form and structure of language relatively independent of the neurological work described in the previous section. Indeed, it would be fair to say that, initially at least, the two approaches represented quite distinct levels of inquiry into the study of language. The psycholinguistic approach is essentially '**top-down**', whereas the neurological approach is very much '**bottom-up**'.

Psycholinguists study a variety of different aspects of language.

- Phonology is the investigation of basic speech sounds ('ba', 'pa' and 'ta' are known as phonemes).
- Phonemes are strung together to form words. We refer to our store of words as our lexicon. (It runs to about 50,000 words for an average adult.)

- Evidence suggests that our lexicon must (in part) be organised in terms of meaning. The study of meaning in language is known as semantics.
- Words are strung together to form sentences according to particular implicit rules of grammar. This involves syntax (*syntactic* is the adjective).
- Finally, the study of using language in a natural social setting is known as pragmatics.

From this summary, you can see that psycholinguistics has a distinct approach and different level of inquiry. However, it is still of interest to ask whether there is any common ground between it and the classic neurological approach. Earlier for example, we noted how Wernicke's and other 'posterior' aphasias involve speech which despite being correctly structured, is difficult or even impossible to understand. There is also poor comprehension. A psycholinguistic interpretation would be that these aphasias are related to *semantic* processing rather than the brain's *syntactic* mechanisms. This would, in turn, imply that semantic processing was a function of these posterior regions.

I earlier described individuals with damage to frontal regions (including Broca's area) as having non-fluent aphasia. In psycholinguistic terms, this type of aphasia could be thought of in terms of impaired *syntactic* processing. We know that some non-fluent aphasics have difficulties in understanding language, which would imply a problem with semantics too. (However, you might remember that these problems only arise where understanding depends on precise grammatical analysis in the absence of other semantic clues. Broca's aphasics would, for example, be able to distinguish between the meaningful sentence 'the boy ate the cake' and the meaningless sentence 'the cake ate the boy'. Actually, they can also distinguish between grammatical and agrammatical sentences.) It seems that the problem for individuals with frontal aphasias such as Broca's is not that grammatical processing mechanisms have been lost; rather, that they cannot be easily accessed. This is the case either for understanding spoken language or for speech. As we shall see, converging evidence indicates that syntax is dealt with in the more anterior/frontal regions.

Neurophysiological approaches

Recently it has become possible to explore some of the ideas that I have described above using CT, MRI and PET (see Chapter 3). These approaches are gradually leading to important discoveries about many aspects of brain function and language is no exception.

CT and MRI scans confirm (in living individuals) the post-mortem findings of extensive damage and loss of tissue to frontal areas in people with Broca's aphasia. They also pinpoint posterior damage in individuals with Wernicke's aphasia (Naeser and Hayward 1978; and Damasio and Damasio 1989). When PET is used to examine brain function, patients with non-fluent (Broca's type) aphasia show underactivation in left-frontal regions, whilst patients with fluent aphasia show underactivation in more posterior regions.

We can also use PET with normal individuals whilst they under-take different types of linguistic task: Petersen and Fiez (1993) asked subjects to perform one of two tasks. In the first, they had to decide whether (or not) pairs of nonsense syllables ended in the same conso-nant (which effectively made the subjects say the words to themselves). In the second, subjects had to interpret grammatically (syntactically) complex sentences. They found that both tasks led to increased activity in and around Broca's area, showing the impor-tance of this cortical region in speech production and grammatical processes.

Raichle (1994) reported what has come to be acknowledged as a classic PET study (which I review in Chapter 8). Amongst other find-ings Raichle's team showed that listening to words activated the left temporal lobe and regions in and around Wernicke's area, whereas having to generate words brought about activation of Broca's area. This strongly supports the involvement of different frontal and poste-rior cortical regions in different linguistic tasks.

Language and laterality

So far, the research I have reviewed suggests that language is mediated by a series of interconnected regions in the left hemisphere. This pattern of 'distributed control' is found in almost all right-handers, and the majority of left-handers. The PET findings from the study by Raichle *et al.* provide very strong evidence that even simple tasks (like the ones used in their study) lead to increased activity in many brain regions especially on the left side. Over 100 years ago Broca wrote 'We speak with our left brain'. Not only do the 'imaging' findings bear this out, but so too does the research on the split brain syndrome and data based on use of the Wada test (both reviewed in Chapter 4).

So can we conclude from these findings that language is exclusively a left-brain function? Not quite: for there is compelling evidence to show that certain *emotional* aspects of language are managed, perhaps predominantly, by the right hemisphere. For example, individuals with right hemisphere damage, and with otherwise intact language skills, may speak in a monotone, despite 'understanding' the emotional connotations of what they are saying. The region of right cortex in question is in the equivalent location to Broca's on the left. In other words, damage to Broca's area impairs fluent speech. Damage to the equivalent area on the right impairs emotionally intoned (**prosodic**) speech, which instead is said to be 'aprosodic'.

Damage further back on the right side (in regions equivalent to Wernicke's area on the left side) can lead to problems relating to the interpretation of emotional tone. Obviously, the actual message often conveys enough meaning to be understood without having to de-code the emotional tone too. But sometimes, appreciation of tone is critical in understanding the true message. 'Thanks very much!' can mean 'thank you' or 'thanks for nothing' depending on the way it is said. The right hemisphere's interpretation of what are known as 'prosodic cues' is closely related to more fundamental skills in detecting tonal differences, or changes to pitch, which are also mediated primarily by the right hemisphere.

Recently, working with colleagues (Stirling *et al.* 1999), we have reported data that is consistent with a left ear (right hemisphere) advantage in normal individuals for the detection of emotional tone in a dichotic listening task, so the effect is not restricted to brain-damaged individuals. Finally, there is circumstantial evidence linking inferential skills (filling in the blanks, or 'putting two and two together') and even 'sense of humour' to the right side too.

Match-up the features of impaired language (1–6) to the different forms of language disorder (a–f):

1. monotone speech
2. widespread language impairment
3. nonsensical speech
4. failure to understand the meaning of specific words
5. telegraphic speech
6. difficulty repeating spoken language

a) Broca's aphasia
b) Wernicke's aphasia
c) conduction aphasia
d) global aphasia
e) pure word deafness
f) aprosody

Summary

The classic neurological approach to understanding the role of the brain in language has relied on case studies of people with localised damage, usually to the left hemisphere. Broca and Wernicke described differing forms of aphasia: the prominent features of the former being non-fluent agrammatical speech, and those of the latter being fluent but usually unintelligible speech. Their work soon led to the development of Lichtheim's 'connectionist' model of language. This emphasised both localisation of function and the connections between functional areas. Connectionist models have continued to be a focus of interest for much of this century. More recently, psycholinguists have drawn attention to the structure of language processes in normal individuals. These distinct approaches, coupled with the use of in-vivo imaging procedures have prompted new ideas about the networks of brain centres that mediate language. Although many of these centres are located in the left hemisphere, interpretation of emotional tone and prosody appear to depend on right hemisphere structures. 'Distributed control' is truly an apt description of the co-ordination of language functions in the brain.

Further reading

Banich M. (1997) *Neuropsychology: The neural bases of mental function*, Boston, MA: Houghton-Mifflin, Chapter 8. A detailed but readable account of the convergence of the connectionist and psycholinguistics approaches to understanding brain function in language. Good summary of in-vivo research too.

Temple, C. (1993) *The Brain*, Penguin: London, Chapter 4. A remarkably effective summary of the classic connectionist model of language in the brain, and a quite detailed introduction to the field of psycholinguistics.

7

Visual mechanisms and perception

Introduction

Of all the senses, vision, in the view of many people, is the most remarkable. Think for a minute of the processing that is required as you read this page. The lines and angles of print reflect light into your eyes. The light excites cells in the retina, which send nerve impulses deep into the brain. From here, the 'neural messages' undergo several further stages of processing. There are separate cortical regions to deal with colour and movement, and additional regions to co-ordinate reading, object recognition and probably facial recognition too. Yet if you close your eyes for a moment, turn round a few times, then open them again, your view of the world is, to all intents and purposes, instantaneous and effortless!

Sensation and perception

To simplify matters, I will distinguish between the *sensory* mechanisms of vision, and the *perceptual* processes which permit recognition of the visual input. 'Visual sensation' is about input 'getting registered' in the brain. Perception is concerned with the interpretation of the stimulus. To understand the former we need to know a little about the structure of the eye, and the route that visual input takes from the retina to the occipital cortex. To understand the latter (or perhaps begin to understand, since so much more is yet to be learned by psychologists), we will consider some research findings from case studies of people who have lost certain perceptual functions, usually after damage or disease to key cortical regions. However, it is important to realise at the outset that the distinction between 'sensation' and 'perception' is, to some extent, arbitrary, because a good deal of 'processing' of visual input takes place almost as soon as light enters the eye. By retaining the distinction, I am, to some extent, following convention as much as good scientific sense.

(The following section provides a sketch of the visual sensory pathways in humans. The next section offers a brief summary of the mechanisms of colour vision. For more detailed information, see the reading at the end of this chapter. If you are more interested in perceptual processing than sensory mechanisms skip to p. 105.)

Sensory processes: from eye to brain

As light enters the eye, it passes through a rather cloudy lens (behind the pupil), and through some dark-coloured fluid which occupies most of the inner space of the eye. Finally it squeezes past several layers of cells (making up the retina) before 'stimulating' the light-sensitive chemicals found in the rods and cones. The image that projects onto the retina is upside down, left–right reversed, and distorted because of the shape of the eye (and lens). It is, in short, a miracle that we ever see anything with such a peculiar sensory structure. (See Figure 7.1a.)

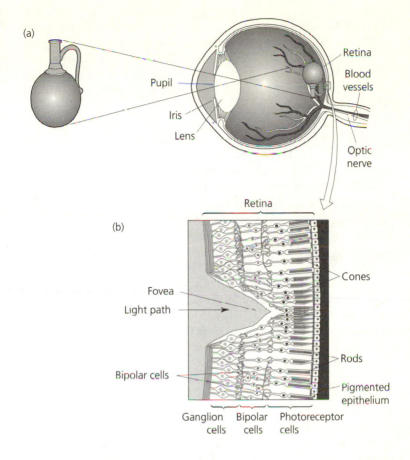

Figure 7.1 **Structure of the human eye**

Source: Rosenzweig *et al.* (1996: 327). Reprinted with permission from Sinauer Associates, Sunderland, MA.

The retina

As I have already said, each retina occupies approximately the back third of the inner wall of the eye. (See Figure 7.1b.) It consists of several layers of cells which 'face backwards'. The cells actually detect the light that bounces off the back wall of the eye, known as the

pigmented epithelium. In the following sections, I will focus on the **rods** and **cones**, the **bi-polar cells** and the **retinal ganglion cells**. However, the retina contains two other types of cell known as amacrine and **horizontal cells**. These are not directly involved in relaying visual input, but they contribute to the formation of receptive fields which I describe briefly below.

Rods and cones   So-called because of their shape, rods and cones are also known as photoreceptors because they are sensitive (receptive) to light (photo). Their ability to respond is made possible because they contain chemicals which are activated by light to produce changes in electrical activity sufficient to stimulate the next layer of cells. Humans have about 100 million rods and 4 million cones per eye.

Most of the cones are found in the fovea, which is the area of the retina that would be stimulated when you look specifically at something. This is a comparatively small region roughly equivalent to the size of your thumb nail with your arm outstretched. There are rods here too, but most rods are found in more peripheral regions of the retina where there are very few cones. Rods are insensitive to colour, but very sensitive to light, and this explains why, at night, you may see a moving light towards the edge of your visual field, but fail to spot it as you direct your gaze towards the source. The distinction also explains why colour vision is so poor at night.

Bi-polar cells   Rods and cones influence bi-polar cells which make up the next layer of the retina. The rods and cones do not act independently, but rather as part of a so-called receptive field. (These result from the convergence of the output of lots of photoreceptors onto far fewer bi-polar cells.) In the fovea receptive fields are small because there is relatively little convergence, so acuity (definition) is high. In the periphery, receptive fields are larger because there is much more convergence. This leads to comparatively lower acuity.

Receptive fields   Think of receptive fields as circles representing different parts of the retina. Research has revealed that each has two distinct regions; a round central area and a doughnut-like surround. However, just to complicate matters, bi-polar cells fall into two classes. Some have receptive fields with 'on-centres' and 'off-surrounds'. This means that a narrow beam of light stimulating the centre area of that receptive field will excite the bipolar cell, whereas the same beam falling on the surround will inhibit it. Other receptive fields have 'off-centres' and 'on-surrounds'! Here, our beam of light will lead to reduced activity if it stimulates the (off) centre, and increased activity if it stimulates the (on) surround. In case you are wondering, when light stimulates both centre and surround regions the net effect will be some excitation for on-centre cells and some inhibition for off-centre cells.

The upshot of this phenomenally complex 'cellular wiring' is that edges and corners of objects are the most clearly defined elements in our visual field. For example, if you were looking at a white square on a dark background, the greatest amount of excitation would occur in the bi-polar cells whose receptive fields received reflected light from the boundary between the square and the background. This is because there is an antagonistic effect between centre and surround which has the effect of 'sharpening' borders. (Actually, it seems likely that our image of the outside world in general is built up mainly from the contours, lines and edges of objects in it.) As you will see, the concept of receptive field is retained and modified at later stages in the pathway.

Retinal ganglion cells   Bi-polar cells either excite or inhibit retinal ganglion cells. However, we must again distinguish between the fovea and the peripheral visual field. In the former, there is little or no convergence. In the periphery, we have already seen that lots of photoreceptors converge on fewer bi-polar cells. It is also the case that several bi-polar cells may converge on a single retinal ganglion cell.

The receptive fields of retinal ganglion cells (like bi-polar cells) are circular, with on or off centres (and off or on surrounds). But in addition to brightness and contrast sensitivity, many retinal ganglion cells that are stimulated by photoreceptors in the fovea are also sensitive specifically to red/green or blue/yellow. You've probably guessed that some have 'red on centres', and 'green off surrounds' ... and so on. This observation has helped us to understand the mechanisms involved in colour vision which I consider briefly below.

The blind spot

The axons of the retinal ganglion cells leave the eye to form the optic nerve (see Figure 7.1a), which in turn becomes the optic tract once it enters the brain. The point where the nerve leaves the eye is known as the blind spot (in effect, a hole in the retina, so there are no rods or cones here). You can find the position of your blind spot by a simple test: close your left eye and look straight ahead at a horizontal line about 50 cm in front of you. Gradually bring the first finger of your right hand into view from the right side, at the same height as the horizontal line you are looking at. You will find that your finger disappears when it is about 15–20 cm to the right of the point you are looking at, and it reappears 1–2 cm later!

In the brain, the optic nerve from each eye divides at a region known as the optic chiasm. Axons from the inner side of the retina (the nasal side) cross, whereas those from the outer side (temporal) stay on the same side. The effect of this is that information from your left visual field (i.e. everything to the left of centre as you look straight ahead) goes to the right side of your brain. Similarly information from your right visual field goes to the left side of your brain. This is seen in Figure 7.2.

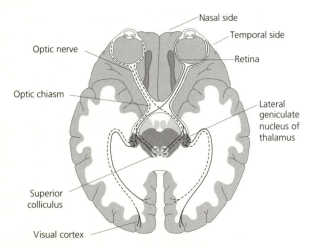

Figure 7.2   **Connections of the human visual system**

Source: Kalat (1995: 187, figure 6.6). Reprinted with permission of Wadsworth Publishing, a division of International Publishing.

The lateral geniculate nucleus (LGN)

The axons of most bi-polar cells terminate in part of the thalamus known as the LGN (see Figure 7.2). Actually, we each have two LGNs; one on each side of the thalamus. The LGN has six distinct layers of cells. Three of the layers receive input from the retina on the opposite side; the other three receive input from the retina on the same side. The retina is 'mapped' out quite precisely (topographically) in each LGN layer, and each layer is 'in register' (synchronised) with the others. So an object in our visual field (seen with both eyes) will activate cells in all six layers of the LGN at precisely the same point.

Livingstone and Hubel (1988) have distinguished between magno and parvocellular LGN cells. The former, comprising the inner two layers, have relatively large receptive fields and are sensitive to movement but not colour. The latter, comprising layers three to six, have much smaller receptive fields and seem to be especially sensitive to form and colour but not movement.

The axons of about 10% of retinal ganglion cells make their way to the superior colliculus which I mentioned in Chapter 2. Their function is not directly related to the process of seeing, but may be linked to the phenomenon of '**blindsight**'. This curious disorder is sometimes observed in individuals who have sustained massive damage to their visual cortex, and are thus, to all intents and purposes 'blind' (i.e. they report being unable to see anything). However, such individuals can sometimes reach accurately for objects and avoid objects that they may otherwise fall over, despite their 'blindness'. The involvement of non-cortical regions in this phenomenon is supported by the observation that damage to either the superior colliculi (located sub-cortically in the mid-brain) or the pathway from the retina to this region eliminates 'blindsight'. (See Figure 7.2.)

The visual cortex

Output from the LGN travels (in the form of action potentials) along the axons of the geniculo-cortical pathway into the primary visual cortex (see Figure 7.2). I will call this region visual area 1 (V1), although some textbooks still use the older name striate cortex.

Much of the pioneering work on visual processing in the cortex was undertaken by Hubel and Weisel who worked mainly with cats (e.g. Hubel and Weisel 1968). They used very simple stimuli such as dots or bars of light, and recorded from V1 cells to see which caused the most response. They soon discovered that dots of light were not effective stimuli for this region, but that slits or bars of light on the other hand caused considerable excitation.

In V1 the cells are organised in columns at right angles to the surface of the cortex, and Hubel and Weisel found that all the cells in a particular column responded to bars of light in the same orientation (i.e. at the same angle). By moving the recording electrode sideways a fraction of a millimetre, another column of cells sensitive to a new orientation could be identified. (So, if a recording electrode was inserted at a shallow angle to the surface of area V1, at different depths it encountered columns sensitive to bars of light oriented at every different angle.) Hubel and Weisel called these orientation-sensitive cells **simple cells**.

When the recording electrodes were moved slightly towards the region of visual cortex now known as V2, Hubel and Weisel found cells that became more excited by bars of light (in a particular orientation) that moved, irrespective of the precise location of the image on the retina. They called these cells **complex cells**, and assumed that they received input from groups of simple cells. Hubel and Weisel also identified some cells as **hypercomplex cells**. They assumed that these cells received their inputs from groups of complex cells, so that they responded best to moving corners, and 'stopped ends'. Hubel and Weisel's model is *hierarchical*. Information is fed forward from simple to complex to hypercomplex cells, which are responsible for the recognition of progressively more sophisticated aspects of the visual input.

Hubel and Weisel in retrospect

In 1981, Hubel and Weisel jointly received the Nobel prize for Physiology and Medicine for their work on perceptual processing in the visual cortex. Unfortunately, although the existence of orientation sensitive cells in V1 had, by then, been confirmed by other researchers, problems were becoming apparent with other parts of Hubel and Weisel's model. One difficulty was that some cells in V2 and even V3, V4 and V5 (visual regions progressively further away from V1) (Figures 7.3a and 7.3b) received information from the LGN as quickly as the simple cells in V1. A second problem was that many

V1 cells were responsive to movement, and colour as well as location. Researchers also realised that the V1 cells that Hubel and Weisel thought were most sensitive to bars or slits of light were actually most sensitive to gratings of light (multiple parallel bars of light and dark of varying width).

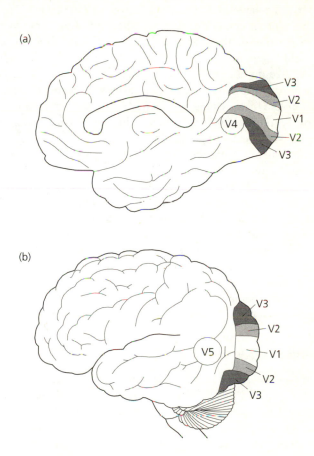

Figure 7.3   **Visual cortical areas in the human brain**

Notes:

(a)   Medial view (from the mid-line looking out)

(b)   Lateral view (from the left side)

Modules in V1

Despite these problems, Hubel and Weisel's work is still acknowledged as both ground breaking and pivotal. From their research, we now have a clearer idea of how area V1 is organised. Researchers think that in humans it is divided into over 2000 units in each hemisphere called **modules**. Each module has about 150,000 neurons, and is dedicated to the analysis of various aspects of visual input in a very small proportion of the visual field, although collectively the entire visual field is represented. If we could flatten out V1, the modules would be like tiny pieces of tile in a massive mosaic. Within V1, a grossly disproportionate area (about 25%) is dedicated to deal with input from the fovea which, as I mentioned earlier represents only a small proportion of your visual field. The rest of your visual field is dealt with by the remaining modules.

Modules all have a common structure. They are three dimensional, and comprise two long thin box-like regions one of which receives input from the left, and the other input from the right eye. In each box, the central area, which runs like a core from the top of the box to the bottom, is circular, and referred to as a '**blob**'. Cells in the blob are sensitive to colour, but not to any other stimulus feature (Livingstone and Hubel, 1988). Cells surrounding the blob (called somewhat unimaginatively the **inter-blob region**) are responsive to orientation, some movement, and to binocular disparity (the difference in image generated by viewing it with both eyes, which contributes to depth perception and probably perception of movement too).

Visual processing beyond V1

After initial processing in V1 the distinction between sensation and perception which I mentioned at the start of this chapter becomes increasingly blurred. Researchers have found at least thirty additional cortical areas responsible for processing different attributes of the visual input. These tend to segregate into two parallel paths of cortical regions known as the WHAT and WHERE streams: the former is concerned with object recognition; the latter object location. I return to consider these in the section on perceptual processes which follows after my summary of colour vision mechanisms.

Colour vision

Sensitivity to the range of colours that humans can detect is a feature of our visual system which we share only with other primates, although most animals are thought to have some rudimentary colour vision (i.e. to restricted parts of the spectrum). Processing of colour occurs at at least four points in the visual pathway we have mapped out:

* the cones are the photoreceptors 'sensitive' to wavelength of light, and hence colour
* many retinal ganglion cells are sensitive to particular colours
* the blobs in V1 are the location of the initial cortical processing of colour input
* V4 is an additional colour vision centre in the WHAT stream

The trichromatic and opponent theories

Most ideas about how the visual system deals with colour have focused on the early stages of the process. The first hypothesis was put forward by Young (1802), and subsequently supported by Helmholtz (1852). It is known as the Young–Helmholtz **trichromatic** hypothesis, and explains colour vision on the basis of there being three distinct colour receptors in the retina, maximally sensitive to blue, green and red hues respectively. Thus a blue object would produce the greatest response in blue receptors, and a purple object would produce responses in red and blue receptors, and so on. According to the theory, colour and brightness are detected in the brain by comparing the relative responses of the three types of cone to particular stimuli.

Hering proposed a different explanation which is known as the 'opponent process theory' because it is based on the idea of opposed colours. He argued that colour vision was built from just three pairs of opposed colours; red–green, blue–yellow, and black–white. Some cells are excited by green and inhibited by red, other excited by blue and inhibited by yellow, and so on. Hering was aware that if you look at a blue image for a minute or so, then turn your gaze to a blank white page, you will see a yellow 'after-image' for a short while. His explanation for this after-image was that during prolonged exposure to a particular colour, the cells most sensitive to that colour gradually become fatigued. When the colour is removed, they no longer inhibit (or oppose) cells sensitive to the opposing colour. As a result these cells become temporarily excited, giving rise to the apparent (opposed) colour.

Evaluation of the trichromatic and opponent theories

Who was right? The answer is that both theories are partly correct, but neither is sufficient by itself. For example, there are three types of cone, one that responds maximally to blue (short wavelengths), another that responds maximally to green (medium wavelengths), and a third that responds maximally to green–yellow–red (long wavelengths) … but none that respond specifically to red. In addition, each type of cone is actually responsive (to some extent) to a range of colours rather than specifically to just one.

One problem for the trichromatic theory is the nature of colour blindness. According to this theory we might expect people with defects to one sort of cone to have colour blindness to one of the principle colours (blue, green or red). In fact, the most common form is red–green colour blindness. This actually means that the person sees his/her world mainly in blues and yellows; even red and green objects appear yellowish. Colour blindness just to blue or green is not found. The colour after-image experience mentioned above is also hard to explain purely in terms of three different types of cone.

What of the opponent theory? There is good evidence in support of this theory at the level of retinal ganglion cells. In humans about 60% of these cells show colour 'opponency'. As I hinted earlier, some retinal ganglion cells tend to be most sensitive to red and green, and others to blue and yellow. The wiring of cones to retinal ganglion cells is very complex, but the upshot is that retinal ganglion cells signal colours to the brain by an 'opponent' mechanism. This provides us with a physiological explanation of the after-image effect that Hering based his theory on: prolonged exposure to one colour really does lead to fatigue in retinal ganglion cells responding to that colour, and compensatory increased activity in cells sensitive to the 'opponent' colour. This activation continues for a while when the observer looks at a blank page, hence the opposite colour after-image.

In summary, there is evidence in support of both the trichromatic and opponent theories. The former accounts for the initial detection of different hues by the three different types of cone. The latter explains the mechanism of many retinal ganglion cells.

Colour perception

The opponent and trichromatic theories are concerned with the sensory registration of colour early on in the visual pathway. However, deficits in colour vision can also occur following damage in areas of visual association cortex, especially to region V4. But now, the nature of the deficit is quite distinct to the forms of colour blindness discussed earlier. With bilateral damage the individual typically loses all colour vision, and his/her visual world becomes monochrome. (Like an old black and white film: the entire visual field appears as various shades of grey). With unilateral damage, the effect is limited to just half the field of vision. Another feature of this disorder, known as **achromatopsia** (Zeki 1992), is that individuals cannot even recall colours from before the time the damage occurred. If the damage is restricted to V4, all other aspects of visual perception remain intact!

Consider each of the following pairs of terms. Draw up a flow diagram linking *one* of each pair into two general strands of visual information processing:

a) fovic region and peripheral region of retina
b) large and small visual fields
c) colour and black/white vision
d) magno and parvo cellular regions of LGN
e) blob and inter-blob regions

Progress exercise

Perceptual processes

The sensory mechanisms considered up to now explain how visual images stimulating photoreceptors in the retina are registered in the brain. So, if we were looking at an object such as a pencil, we know that certain cells in our primary visual cortex would be activated by the lines, angles and shadings (the physical features) of the image. This, of course, is some way removed from the 'realisation' that the object is a pencil; that it needs regular sharpening; and that it can be used to write or draw with. To understand a little of how *perception* occurs, we must move beyond the sensory registration stages and consider additional stages of visual information processing beyond V1 and V2.

The separation of sensory and perceptual processes is clearly illustrated if the pencil is rotated: As it moves, quite different populations of cortical neurons will be stimulated, *yet a rotating pencil is still perceived as a pencil!* Similarly, if the pencil was now in someone's hand, and the person was drawing a simple shape, even if s/he was facing you, and thus the drawing was upside down, you would probably be able to recognise what was being drawn. Recognition would (at the very least) require the mental rotation of the sketch through 180°.

The WHAT and WHERE streams and visual perception

As I mentioned in the previous section, two major streams of perceptual processing have been identified; one for object recognition, which I have referred to as the WHAT stream, and a second for recognition of spatial relationships which I have called the WHERE stream. Each stream obviously starts in the occipital cortex, but the WHAT stream takes a ventral (round the side) route into the temporal lobes, whereas the WHERE stream takes a more dorsal route (over the top of the brain) into the parietal lobes.

Output to be dealt with in the WHAT route travels via V2 and V4 into the temporal lobes. As we have already seen, cells in V4 provide a good example of the type of higher level perceptual processing that we find in the WHAT stream: V4 cells seem to be tuned to particular colours irrespective of stimulus orientation, location or movement. Output along the WHERE route travels via V2 and V3 into area V5, and then into the parietal and (medial) temporal lobes. V5 provides a second example of higher order processing (in the WHERE stream). Here we find cells that are exquisitely sensitive to stimuli moving in a particular direction at a particular speed irrespective of their exact location in the visual field. (See Figure 7.3a and b.)

Object recognition: the WHAT stream and agnosia

The recognition of objects depends on cortical processing in the ventral stream running from the primary visual cortex into the temporal lobes. When, for example, we record the 'firing patterns' of cells along this route (i.e. what stimuli excite them), we find that relatively simple stimuli lead to excitation of cells early on in the route (i.e. still close to the primary visual cortex). However, more specific and complex stimuli must be shown to make later cells fire. Remarkable as it may seem, cells towards the front parts of the temporal lobe (the anterior and polar regions as they are known) only respond to very specific shapes of stimuli such as a hand, or even a particular face. (These cells were once dubbed '**grandmother cells**', because researchers speculated light-heartedly and incorrectly that the ability to recognise one's grandmother depended on one particular cell being excited!).

Additionally, the further forward one looks along this stream, the less important is the physical position of the object in the visual field. (We could describe the cells in these forward regions as having large receptive fields, and in some cases, the entire retina appears to be covered.) So, no matter where the object falls on the retina, cortical cells will respond to (i.e. be excited by) the object (assuming they are tuned to it in the first place). In order to understand better the sort of processing that occurs in this stream, it is helpful to consider some classic neurological disorders which appear to stem from dysfunction or damage to it.

Visual agnosia

In the 1890s, on the basis of a detailed case-study, Lissauer reported two forms of object recognition failure, which he called **apperceptive** and **associative agnosia**. One hundred or so years on, we know that the two disorders are linked to damage to different components of the WHAT stream, and reflect different types of perceptual disturbance. Although there is still some debate about the extent to which apperceptive and associative agnosia overlap, the distinction is generally regarded as helpful and I will retain it.

Apperceptive agnosia   When shown a photograph of a pencil, someone with this type of agnosia will probably be able to describe some of the physical features of it such as its general shape, the point at one end, the ridges down the side and so on. However, they will be quite unable to identify or name the object. Obviously, the degree of impairment depends on the extent of damage, but in the worst cases, when damage to occipital and surrounding posterior regions in the right hemisphere is widespread, apperceptive agnosics cannot even copy simple shapes, or discriminate between them. With more discrete damage, an affected individual may be able to recognise an object if viewed from a typical position, but be unable to recognise the same object if it is viewed from an unusual perspective.

People with apperceptive agnosia are unable to put individual parts of a visual stimulus *together* to form what psychologists call a '**percept**'. We know that the problem is 'perceptual' rather than 'sensory' because apperceptive agnosics can describe individual elements of an object. However, according to Warrington (1982) this form of agnosia is related to an early stage in perceptual processing which involves the linking of perceptual inputs with stored images of objects. (This process is essential for proper perception, in order to overcome inevitable perceptual variability in visual stimuli when viewed at different angles, distances, or perspectives.) Apperceptive agnosia occurs because of damage at an early stage in the ventral processing stream. It is found in individuals who have sustained damage to the posterior regions of the right hemisphere.

Associative agnosia   Individuals with this form of agnosia can copy objects relatively well, and detect similar items from a display. In some cases, they may even be able to sort items into groupings (animals, items of cutlery, tools, etc). The problem in associative agnosia is an inability to identify (and name) the object in question.

Consider the following situation: a patient is shown an assortment of cutlery. He picks up a fork, and, when asked, draws a recognisable sketch of it. (This shows that perception of the item is relatively complete.) He may, if asked, be able to find another similar item from the cutlery draw. However, he would still be unable to identify the item as a fork! Moreover, if later asked to draw the object from memory, he would be unable to do so, although if actually asked to draw a fork, he probably could. Even at this point, he will not realise that the object he was holding and the drawing he has just made were of the same item!

Another insight into the cognitive deficit found in associative agnosia is provided by the work of Warrington and her colleagues. In one study by Warrington and Taylor (1978) agnosics had to match objects according to function. They were shown a picture of a particular object, such as a rolled-up umbrella, and two other objects (an open umbrella, and a walking stick) from which to choose a match. The correct functional match would be the open umbrella, but people with associative agnosia usually chose the walking stick (which looked more similar). This shows that the core problem in associative agnosia is in *linking percepts to meaning*. Object recognition is certainly more complete than for someone with apperceptive agnosia. However, the remaining problem is one of forming links between the 'percept' and stored semantic information about such items. This may be related to damage to semantic systems in the left hemisphere or to damage to the pathways connecting the occipito-temporal border regions of the right and left hemispheres.

Recognition of faces and prosopagnosia

Facial recognition is a skill that has long intrigued psychologists, in part because humans seem to be so good at it! Consider the following lines of evidence. Firstly, humans have a phenomenal memory for faces. You will probably have experienced that moment of recognition as you glimpse the face of someone you haven't seen for many years. (I still occasionally recognise people I went to primary school with!) Secondly, research indicates that humans can memorise and learn face information very quickly and with very little effort. People tested using Warrington's facial memory test, in which they look briefly at 50 anonymous black and white photographs of people, can correctly recognise most or all of them in a later test. Thirdly, although the distinctions between faces are subtle (all humans have eyes, nose and mouth), humans are able to scan large numbers of photographs very quickly to find the one famous face in the crowd.

Psychologists interested in evolutionary aspects of behaviour have made the point that historically, it must have been especially important for humans to be able to recognise friend from foe, or kin from neighbour. Specialised brain regions, they suggest, will have evolved to facilitate such 'innate' skills. However, not all psychologists agree. Some argue that despite the intuitive appeal of this idea, the processing of faces is really just a very sophisticated form of object recognition, and that we are good at it because we have lots of practice! In their review of the literature Kolb and Whishaw (1996) came down in favour of this viewpoint.

A small number of people suffer from a form of visual agnosia which involves the inability to perceive faces. In **prosopagnosia** the degree of impairment is, as with object recognition, variable. In some cases, patients may be unable to match pairs of faces, or say whether two photographs are of the same individual. In other cases, these perceptual skills appear to be intact, but recognition of particular individuals such as film stars or even members of the person's own family may be affected. In the most extreme and perplexing form of the disorder, the person may even lose the ability to recognise themselves from photographs or in the mirror.

Many people with prosopagnosia also show other abnormalities of object recognition; a finding which suggests that prosopagnosia may just be a type of object recognition failure after all. However, several individuals have now been studied in which there is *a double dissociation* between object recognition and facial recognition. This suggests that facial recognition is a separate skill that need not overlap with object recognition. In one case reported by McNeil and Warrington (1993), a farmer learned to identify individual sheep in his flock after becoming prosopagnosic for human faces!

Two further lines of enquiry also point towards the involvement of special brain mechanisms in face recognition. If we consider the question of location of brain damage and prosopagnosia, the following picture emerges. Most cases have experienced bilateral damage, and this is predominantly to occipital or temporal lobes. Of those prosopagnosics with unilateral lesions, the vast majority have incurred damage to the right hemisphere, again mainly to occipital and/or temporal regions. In fact Farah (1990) could find only four cases (6% of her sample) of prosopagnosia following unilateral left-sided damage. Overall, this is quite strong evidence of a specialised role for the right hemisphere in face recognition

The other supportive line of evidence comes from studies of object and face recognition using PET in normal individuals. In a study by Sergent *et al.* (1992), the researchers found several regions in both hemispheres that became active when subjects completed tests of face and object recognition. However, when subjects had to group photographs of people by sex, only the occipital/temporal regions of the right hemisphere were activated. And proper face identification activated temporal regions further forward in the right hemisphere only. This ties in with the finding that cells towards the front of the temporal lobe seem to be especially sensitive to person-related items including faces (recall the case of grandmother cells).

In summary, the available evidence suggests that face recognition *is* more than just a sophisticated form of object recognition. Prosopagnosia seems to be linked to damage to the specialised brain regions that normally deal with faces. These areas include ventral (side) regions of occipital and temporal lobes on the right side. One interpretation of the data is that posterior regions (early in the WHAT stream) deal with the integrative process of putting together the face from its component parts. However, areas further forward, but still on the right side, are concerned with identification, and linking this with other semantic and biographic information about that person.

Box 7.1: A case study of prosopagnosia

THERAPIST (*shows patient a picture of a cow and horse*) Which is the horse?

PATIENT That's easy … the one on the right without horns.

THERAPIST (*shows photograph of Elvis Presley*) Do you know who this is?

PATIENT Is it a famous person?

THERAPIST Yes.

PATIENT Is it the Pope?

THERAPIST No, this person is no longer alive … Describe the face to me.

PATIENT Well, he's tall, and got black hair swept back with lots of grease …

THERAPIST Does he have a moustache?

PATIENT No, but he has long sideburns ... and a guitar.

THERAPIST It's Elvis Presley! (*patient nods, but doesn't appear to connect the face to the name*)

THERAPIST Now, who's this? (*shows photograph of patient's wife*)

PATIENT I dunno ... some woman ... about my age with grey hair and nice eyes ...

THERAPIST It's your wife. (*patient once again seems unable to connect the picture to the identification*)

THERAPIST Okay. Who's this? (*shows photograph of patient*)

PATIENT No idea ...

THERAPIST Describe him ...

PATIENT Well, he looks quite old, and has lost a lot of hair. He looks like he needs a holiday, with those bags under his eyes ... A good long rest ...

THERAPIST It's you!

PATIENT No... you are kidding me! It's a very poor photograph. I don't look a bit like that!

Evaluation of the WHAT stream and agnosia

I have presented the WHAT stream as a sort of route along which visual information must pass in order for object recognition to occur. It includes a large area of the ventral (side) regions of cortex on both sides of the brain. In general terms it seems that regions further away from V1 deal with progressively more subtle aspects of recognition.

Object recognition is clearly linked to perception rather than sensation. However, it probably involves several stages, and specialised faculties seem to be built into the stream. Apperceptive agnosia results from problems that occur relatively 'early on' in perceptual processing. The individual struggles to put together the 'whole' (the percept) from its component parts. Associative agnosia must reflect damage further along in the processing stream because the percept seems reasonably well formed. Here the problem is one of linking the percept to meaning. Some psychologists think that face recognition is just a particular form of object recognition, but most now regard prosopagnosia as a disorder to a specialised faculty (for face recognition) within the WHAT stream. Converging evidence identifies regions towards the front of the right temporal lobe that may be involved in this aspect of perception.

Spatial functions and the WHERE stream

Earlier in this chapter, I said that researchers had evidence for both a WHAT and a WHERE stream of perceptual processing. The agnosic conditions reviewed in the previous sections illustrate the effects of disturbances to the functioning of the WHAT (perhaps it should be what and who) stream, but we now need to consider the other stream, which is concerned with spatial functions.

The WHERE stream takes a more 'northerly' route forward from the occipital cortex, entering the parietal lobe, and running further forward into parts of both the frontal and temporal lobe (albeit the medial parts of the temporal lobe usually hidden from view). The right hemisphere is often referred to as the spatial hemisphere, although the left hemisphere also has a number of spatial responsibilities. In the following sections I briefly consider some basic spatial processes related to perception. Next I consider the ability to generate spatial objects, or negotiate routes. Finally, I consider some disturbances to spatial functioning.

Spatial skills related to perception

Localising points in space   Individuals with damage to superior (top most) regions of parietal cortex have difficulty reaching towards a visual stimulus. Left-sided damage affects ability to reach towards the right side, and vice versa. If we remove the movement component, and simply measure perception of left- or right-side space (i.e. detection of stimuli in the left or right visual fields), we find that unilateral damage to the right parietal regions is most likely to affect this skill adversely.

Depth perception   Local depth perception, the ability to detect depth because of the different images falling on each eye (binocular disparity), can be disrupted by both right and left hemisphere lesions.

Line orientation and geometric relations   The ability to judge angles or orientations of lines is affected following right (but not left) parietal damage. Similarly, the ability to remember novel complex shapes of geometric patterns (that cannot be named) is also affected after right parietal damage.

Motion   It is very rare for humans to lose their ability to detect motion, yet retain other perceptual abilities. In the handful of well-documented cases, there is usually damage to both left and right parietal lobes.

Rotation   Both PET research with normal subjects engaged in tasks that involve mental rotation, and analysis of the performance of brain damaged subjects on similar tasks, once again points to the involvement of the right parietal lobe. In a classic study by Deutsch *et al.* (1988) subjects had to decide which hand a 'cartoon man' was holding a ball in. The cartoon was shown in various orientations, and in front and rear view. Patients with right hemisphere lesions made more errors and had slower reaction times on this task.

Spatial skills related to constructional skills

Constructional skills are more complex than the spatial–perceptual tests mentioned above. They involve spatial perception, but in addition require the production or generation of some tangible output. There are several standard neuropsychological assessments of these skills and evidence suggests that right parietal damage is most likely to impair performance on them. However, some caution is required in interpreting test results because, in moving away from the purely perceptual, we introduce other psychological factors. The following two tests certainly involve hand–eye co-ordination and attention, and arguably even memory, (which depend on other cortical functions) in addition to spatial skills.

The *Rey-Osterreith complex figure* is a detailed line drawing which looks a little like the union jack flag, with other elements such as extra triangles and lines attached (see Figure 7.4a). The subject simply has to copy the figure. Normal individuals often complete this task almost faultlessly within a few minutes. However, the apparently straightforward task seems almost impossible for patients with damage in the right temporo-parietal region. Damage in this region also adversely affects individuals on the *block design test* (a test taken from the WAIS) in which subjects have to copy a simple pattern by assembling coloured blocks (see Figure 7.4b). Having used each of these tests in my own research, it really is astonishing to see how difficult some otherwise behaviourally normal individuals find them.

Route finding

For some psychologists the ability to get from point A to B is the very essence of a spatial skill, and once again, there is good evidence that right parietal damage can affect this ability. Researchers have developed a number of tests to assess route finding. They range from simple finger mazes (where a blindfolded subject has to learn a route by trial and error, usually by guiding his finger through a small maze), to following directions using standardised maps. As with the construction tests mentioned above, we must, in interpreting results, be aware that the different tasks assess other skills in addition to basic spatial skills. Moreover, depending on the particular task, it may be possible to use non-spatial strategies as well as, or instead of, spatial ones, which further complicates interpretation.

A variant of the finger maze is where the subject has to find their way through a proper maze. In the maze test devised by Semmes *et al.* (1955), nine dots are placed on the floor of a large room and the subject given a plan of the route (via the dots) they must follow. For reference one wall of the room is designated 'north', and the person is not allowed to rotate the map as they follow the route. Typically, right parietal damage affects performance on this test.

In Money's (1976) standardised road map test, subjects are given a fictitious map which shows a route marked on it. At every junction, they must 'say' which direction (left, right, straight on) to go in. This test requires planning and memory as well as spatial skill, and performance is affected by damage to the frontal areas of the right hemisphere in addition to the more posterior parietal regions. Finally, there is even some evidence that basic geographic knowledge about whole countries or even continents is adversely affected following right-sided damage.

Taken together, these findings illustrate the range of spatial perceptual abilities which humans possess, and which we take for

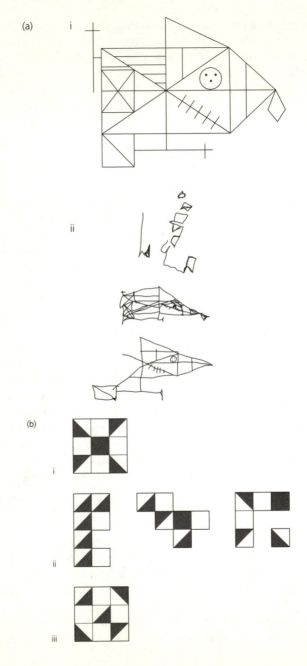

Figure 7.4 (opposite) **Spatial constructional impairments**

Source: Benowitz *et al.* (1990). Reproduced with permission from Cambridge University Press.

Notes:

(a) (i) The Rey-Osterreith complex figure. (ii) Examples of attempts to copy this figure by three individuals with damage to posterior sections of the right hemisphere.

(b) The block design test of spatial construction. (i) An example design that individuals must copy. (ii) Three attempts to copy the design by a person with right-hemisphere damage. (iii) An attempt to copy the design by a person with left hemisphere damage. The overall configuration is right, but the details are incorrect.

granted until a problem arises. Spatial perception depends on the ability to form an internal representation of the outside world, and to locate oneself in it! The formation of that internal representation, and the ability to manipulate it or 'mentally' move around it, depends on effective processing in the WHERE stream.

Specific disorders of spatial processing

We cannot leave the area of spatial functions without brief mention of two specific disorders; Balint's syndrome and hemineglect, which illustrate the importance of intact spatial functioning for normal behaviour.

Balint's syndrome

In this rare disorder, the patient seems to have a sort of tunnel vision, at least in the sense that they can only 'see' one (usually tiny) element of their visual field at any one time. However, unlike tunnel vision, which usually occurs as a result of damage to the retina and means that only the fovic part is functional, Balint's patients can, in fact, view objects anywhere in the visual field. Unfortunately, they cannot easily direct their attention to other parts of it. The Balint's patient is neither retinally nor cortically blind: he or she simply cannot construct an effective 'whole' picture of the spatial world. A classic test for this disorder is to show a picture which tells a story; for example, a car crashing into a tree. The Balint's patient will, with effort, be able to describe individual elements of the picture, but be unlikely ever to understand the whole story. Balint's syndrome is usually found in individuals who have incurred extensive bilateral damage to regions of occipital and parietal cortex.

Hemineglect

In this most bizarre disorder, individuals appear indifferent towards, and sometimes in denial of, half of their visual world. Rarely, this may even extend to denial about their own body: Sacks (1985) reported one hemineglect patient, who, on waking, attempted to throw his own leg out of bed believing it to be a severed leg put there as a cruel joke whilst he was asleep! Usually, this condition results from right-sided parietal damage, and affects perception of the left side or visual field. If asked to draw a clock face, the indifference or inattention to the left visual field will be apparent in the arrangement of all the figures and the clock fingers on the right side of the clock face. The hemineglect patient 'knows' there should be 12 numbers, but these get squeezed to the right side.

Evaluation of spatial perception and the WHERE stream

A quite different set of perceptual skills depend on perceptual processing in the WHERE stream. As we saw with the WHAT stream and object recognition, disturbance or damage to different stages in the WHERE stream can lead to different disturbances in spatial perception. Psychologists have observed a number of deficits in spatial perception linked to this route: mental rotation and localising objects in space would be just two examples. A more sophisticated sort of spatial dysfunction is observed in tasks concerned with route finding, or map reading. Problems with this sort of task are linked to right-sided lesions in several locations within the dorsal stream. Finally, Balint's syndrome and hemineglect reveal that inattention to particular regions of space leads to an inability to comprehend spatial relations in that region.

a) Describe three abnormalities linked to damage to the WHAT stream, and three abnormalities linked to damage to the WHERE stream. Write a brief paragraph of no more than 75 words on each.

b) What, for the psychologist, is the potential problem in setting subjects spatial tasks to do that may be 'solved' using different strategies?

Summary

In the opening passages of this chapter, I reviewed the visual pathway from eye to brain, and considered two theories of colour vision. Visual sensory processing begins in the retina, continues in the lateral geniculate nucleus and concludes in the cortex. In the primary visual cortex, cell assemblies or 'modules' have been identified that attend to very discrete regions of the retina. Even so, different cells within modules seem to be sensitive to colour, brightness and orientation. Other visual areas beyond V1 code for other aspects of visual perception such as colour, form and movement.

Perception of objects depends on activity in two separate processing streams. The WHAT stream deals with object recognition and links with stored memories of related objects. The WHERE stream deals with various aspects of spatial processing, both of perceived objects, and of the individual in space. This distinction is apparent if you consider the situation of reaching to select a particular object from a group of items. The WHERE stream guides your hand to the object, and the WHAT stream allows you to select the right object. The visual agnosias can be understood in terms of disturbances to different stages of processing in the WHAT stream. Balint's syndrome and hemineglect are rare but dramatic examples of neurological disorders which affect different aspects of spatial perception.

Further reading

Gazzaniga, M.S., Ivry, R.B. and Mangun, G.R. (1998) *Cognitive Neuroscience: the Biology of the Mind*, London: Norton, chapters 4 and 5. Superb comprehensive up-to-date summary of the visual pathways with excellent illustrations and figures.

Kolb, B. and Whishaw, I.Q. (1996) *Fundamentals of Human Neuropsychology*, 4th edn, Freeman: New York, chapter 19 (and parts of 20). Comprehensive review of the role of the parietal lobes in perception, with many clinical examples of damage leading to impaired perception.

8

Three research reports

Introduction

In this chapter I present brief summaries of three research reports. I have chosen these carefully from a potentially enormous range of neuroscience and neuropsychology investigations. Each has already been mentioned, often several times in the main text of this book. Each also represents something of a milestone in the particular area under investigation. The report by Mogilner *et al.* (1993) shows that the human somatosensory cortex is, under certain circumstances, capable of astonishing feats of rewiring. This cortical region was once thought to be '**hard-wired**', but studies such as Mogilner's indicate that it has the capacity for '**plastic**' changes well into adulthood and maturity. I have included a summary of some of the work of Raichle's research group (the Petersen *et al.* paper) because this study was one of the first well-controlled PET investigations to examine the anatomical location of various language skills in the brain. The rather more modest study by Delis *et al.* (1986) is included, in part, to illustrate how it is sometimes possible to test very sophisticated psychological theories using simple apparatus and equipment. The findings from this study have led to increased interest in the 'processing styles' theory of lateralisation.

Report 1

'**Somatosensory cortical plasticity in adult humans revealed by magnetoencephalography**', A. Mogilner, J.A., Grossman, U. Ribary, M. Joliot, J. Volkman, D. Rapaport, R.W. Beasley and R.R. Llinas in *Proceedings of the National Academy of Sciences* (1993) 90, 3593–7.

Introduction The topographic representation found in the primary somatosensory cortex is quite consistent from one person to the next. However, recent research with other primates has suggested that in the event of some change to sensory input (through damage to or lesioning of a pathway for example) changes in topographic representation may occur, even in mature organisms. For example, Mersenich and Kaas (1980) showed that in macaques, the hand is precisely mapped in distinct adjacent assemblies of cells in the somatosensory strip. If one digit is removed in infancy or early adulthood, the cortex that would have dealt with sensory input from that finger begins to respond (over a period of months) to input from other digits. In other words, the cortex is not wasted. It becomes absorbed into adjacent cortical regions making them more sensitive.

Mogilner and colleagues were interested to know if similar 'plastic' changes could be observed in adult humans. Obviously, the researchers could not 'lesion' fingers in human subjects! Instead, they recruited two subjects with *syndactyly*; a congenital disorder in which the fingers are malformed and fused together. The researchers recorded activity in the 'hand' region of the primary somatosensory cortex of these subjects before, and again after surgery to 'free' their fused fingers.

METHOD Mogilner *et al.* (1993) used MEG (see Chapter 3) to establish functional activity of the hand region in the somatosensory cortex of their two syndactyly cases, and a group of nine normal control subjects. The researchers were able to map out the regions of cortex that were sensitive to inputs from each finger, even in the syndactyly cases.

The two subjects with syndactyly underwent additional MEG a short while after surgery to separate their fused fingers.

RESULTS Prior to surgery, the cortical mapping of the hand region in the two syndactyly cases was quite distinct and unusual in comparison to the controls. Examination of pre- and post-operative MEG maps indicated marked reorganisation in the cortical hand area in these two cases. In each the result of reorganisation now more closely resembled the cortical maps of controls. The changes were apparent within 1 week, and further MEGs recorded 3 and 6 weeks later indicated relatively little additional change. The re-mapping occurred over distances of between 5 and 10 mm.

DISCUSSION This study is the first to illustrate that functional mapping in the human somatosensory cortex is not, as was once believed, 'hard-wired'. On the contrary, areas of cortex responsive to input from individual fingers 'appear' to move within a few days of surgery. Clearly, the cortex does not actually move, but new regions up to 10 mm away from the original site now seem to respond to sensory input from the newly freed fingers.

It is important to remember that the study is based on just two individuals who had the abnormality from birth. However, in certain respects this makes the speed of change all the more remarkable. Scientists are now trying to identify the mechanisms that permit such re-mapping to occur. The growth of new axons has been suggested, but can be ruled out because of the speed with which the effect was observed: axons do not grow this quickly!

This is important research because it may lead to the development of new strategies to help people recover lost function after nerve damage. In general Mogilner *et al.*'s study is a further reminder of the potential for plastic change present even in the mature cortex.

Report 2

'Positron emission tomographic studies of the cortical anatomy of single word processing', S.E. Petersen, P.T. Fox, M.I. Posner, M. Mintun and M. Raichle in *Nature* (1988) 331, 585–9.

Introduction   Raichle and his group have been exploring the involve-ment of different cortical (and sub-cortical) structures that are active in various types of language-related tasks for some time. By using PET, the group have been able to show which cortical regions become most active during different types of task.

METHOD   Subjects were normal volunteers with no known language impairments. There were four conditions in the study; each under-taken whilst the subject lay in the scanner. In condition one, subjects lay passively in a PET scanner looking at a fixation point on a screen. In condition two, subjects listened passively to a series of nouns, or observed a similar series of nouns displayed on a TV monitor. In condition three, subjects had to repeat aloud the words they heard or saw. Finally, in condition four, subjects had to generate (and speak aloud) a 'related' verb for every noun they heard or saw. Words were presented at the rate of about one every two seconds, so this was a very demanding condition.

Posner and Raichle used what is known as 'subtraction-logic' to generate PET images. In simple terms this means that the PET activity during the control condition is (literally) subtracted by the computer from the activity during the task so that any remaining activity can be attributed to the specific features of the task. Thus, for example, the PET activity produced when subjects repeated words was subtracted from the activity when subjects generated verbs. In this way the researchers could be sure that the remaining activity was linked to the process of generation rather than simply repetition/verbalisation.

RESULTS   As we might expect the two passive conditions of seeing and hearing words activated quite distinct cortical regions. Viewing words led to greatest activation bilaterally in the primary and secondary visual areas. Hearing words led to bilateral activation in the primary and secondary auditory areas in the temporal lobes, and unilaterally on the left side in Wernicke's area. The hearing condition then served as control for the word repetition condition. Now, there was bilateral activation in the motor cortex and SMA controlling face and mouth, and some other regions more usually related to attention than language. In condition four (for which condition three served as control), there was activation of Broca's and Wernicke's areas, and two additional regions which had not hitherto been identified as important language centres: the cingulate and the cerebellum.

DISCUSSION   This research project adds to a growing list of in-vivo imaging studies conducted with normal volunteers rather than neurologically damaged cases. The PET scans support the classic connectionist view of interconnected language centres with specific and distinct responsibilities. However, to some extent, the study also illustrates the weakness of a strict localisationist theory of brain–language function: despite the relatively straightforward nature of the tasks, each appeared to induce activity in many cortical areas. The established regions were activated, but so too were other regions such as the cingulate, which is more normally associated with attention, and the cerebellum which is usually associated with motor learning. Areas in the left hemisphere that had not previously been identified as 'language areas' were also activated, and further PET studies are ongoing to establish the role(s) of these new regions in language.

Report 3

'Hemispheric specialisation of memory for visual hierarchical stimuli', D.C. Delis, L.C. Robertson and R. Efron in *Neuropsychologia* (1986) 24 (2), 205–16.

Introduction   To what extent does selective damage to either the right or left hemisphere affect memory for stimuli comprising larger forms (such as capital letters) made from smaller forms (such as tiny circles)? This was the question that this research team set out to address. The reason for this was that earlier research by Sergent (1982) (which I described in Chapter 4) had characterised the left hemisphere as analytic (interested in fine detail) and the right hemisphere as holistic (more interested in the 'big picture'). Sergent's work involved normal (non-brain damaged) participants responding to stimuli presented very briefly using a tachistoscope. Delis and his colleagues realised that an ideal test of Sergent's hypothesis would be to use similar stimuli with patients who had incurred damage to just one side of the brain, to see whether or not the same hemispheric divisions of labour could be observed.

METHOD Three groups of participants were recruited; 8 individuals with left hemisphere damage, 8 with right hemisphere damage and 8 controls. The stimuli comprised figures, some of which were letters, and others which were simple geometric drawings (e.g. two intersecting lines). Each figure was actually made up of several tiny but recognisable figures. For example a capital 'F' may actually be made up of about 12–15 tiny squares or question marks; the intersecting lines may actually comprise two rows of tiny circles ... etc.

Forty stimuli were used, each being presented for 2 seconds. After each presentation, there was an unrelated 'distraction' task lasting 15 seconds intended to prevent rehearsal. Subjects then had to recognise which object they had just seen from an array of four alternatives.

RESULTS The most important finding to emerge from this study was the difference in recognition rate between subjects for the large and small components of the figures. Participants with left hemisphere damage made more errors recognising the correct small components of figures. (This was even more marked if the small components happened to be tiny letters). Right hemisphere damaged individuals made more errors recognising the larger figures. This difference was statistically highly significant.

DISCUSSION The results of this study confirm and add to the findings of Sergent (1982). Whereas Sergent's study recorded recognition speeds in normal subjects, Delis *et al.* showed that the same basic hemispheric specialisations or responsibilities affect memory for visual stimuli in unilaterally damaged individuals. The findings suggest that people with left hemisphere damage, and who thus rely on right hemisphere processing, neglect the 'small-print' ... the fine detail (so-to-speak). Individuals with right hemisphere damage have the reverse pattern of inattention, leading to memory impairment for the large figures, with retention of memory for the small detail.

Although the authors themselves avoided using the terms *analytic* and *holistic* to describe the processing styles (and in this case memory skills) of the left and right hemispheres respectively, with hindsight, these terms seem quite appropriate. They have certainly been used in this context by other psychologists.

9

Study aids

IMPROVING YOUR ESSAY WRITING SKILLS

At this point in the book you have acquired the knowledge necessary to tackle the exam itself. Answering exam questions is a skill which this chapter shows you how to improve. Examiners have some ideas about what goes wrong in exams. Most importantly, students do not provide the kind of evidence the examiner is looking for. A grade C answer is typically accurate and reasonably constructed but has limited detail and commentary. To lift such an answer to a grade A or B may require no more than fuller detail, better use of material and a coherent organisation. By studying the essays presented in this chapter, and the examiner's comments, you can learn how to turn grade C answers into grade A. Please note that marks given by the examiner in the practice essays should be used as a guide only and are not definitive. They represent the 'raw marks' given by an AEB examiner. That is, the marks the examiner would give to the examining board based on a total of 24 marks per question broken down into Skill A (description) and Skill B (evaluation). Tables showing this scheme are in Appendix C of Paul Humphreys' title in this series, *Exam Success in AEB Psychology*. They may not be the marks given on the examination certificate received ultimately by the student because all examining boards are required to use a common standardised system called the Uniform Mark Scale (UMS) which adjusts all raw scores to a single standard acceptable to all examining boards.

The essays are about the length a student would be able to write in 35–40 minutes (leaving you extra time for planning and checking). Each essay is followed by detailed comments about its strengths and weaknesses. The most common problems to look out for are:

- Failure to answer the actual question set and presenting 'one written during your course'.
- A lack of evaluation, or commentary – many weak essays suffer from this.
- Too much evaluation and not enough description. Description is vital in demonstrating your knowledge and understanding of the selected topic.
- Writing 'everything you know' in the hope that something will get credit. Excellence is displayed through selectivity, and therefore improvements can often be made by *removing* material which is irrelevant to the question set.

For more ideas on how to write good essays you should consult *Exam Success in AEB Psychology* (Paul Humphreys) in this series.

Practice essay 1

(a) **Describe two research studies that have been conducted on 'split brain' patients. (12 marks)**
(b) **Assess the contributions of such studies for our understanding of the localisation of function in the brain. (12 marks)** **[AEB January 1997]**

Candidate's answer to (a)

Para 1: Split brain patients have undergone surgery to divide the two halves of their brains. This used to be a common operation to cure epilepsy, but is not done much these days because drugs are much more effective than they used to be. When patients had got over their operation, it seemed that their general psychological functioning had improved significantly, and scientists concluded that the main job of the corpus callosum was just to hold the two sides of the brain together. However, a team of psychologists did some experiments to reveal the true nature of the split brain syndrome. I will describe the studies by 1. Gazzaniga and Sperry, and 2. Levy *et al.*

Para 2: Gazzaniga and Sperry presented stimuli to split brain subjects one hemisphere at a time. They used a tachistoscope to present pictures or words to either the left or right eye, (which project to the right or left brain respectively). If they presented a picture of a pencil to the right eye, the subjects could identify it, and say what it was, but they couldn't say what it was if it went to the left eye, because this projected to the mute right hemisphere. However they did 'know' it was there because they could draw it with their right hand.

Para 3: Interestingly, if the patient reached behind a screen with either hand they would be able to find the pencil from amongst an array of items, despite claiming not to have seen it, yet they still could not identify it verbally!

Para 4: Levy and colleagues also used a tachistoscope to present 'impossible faces' to subjects. The faces were combinations of two different people who looked quite similar. When subjects were asked what they had seen, they always reported seeing the face on the right. However, when they had to choose which face they saw from a selection of 'whole' faces, they always chose the one that had been presented to the left, going to the right brain.

Candidate's answer to (b)

Para 5: These studies show us that the left and the right side of the brain are specialised for different functions; i.e. that certain tasks are localised within one or other hemisphere. In this respect they add considerably to a growing body of research which shows that language is a left-brain skill, and that spatial functions are dealt with by the right brain.

Para 6: From Gazzaniga and Sperry's study we see that the connections between the eye and brain are very specific, and that if information only gets to the right brain the left brain does not know about it, and therefore cannot describe it. This shows that language is localised to the left brain. Further proof of this idea is that words presented to the right eye can be read without difficulty, and the left hand can also select relevant items from behind a screen. Obviously the person may be a bit confused about the procedure, but generally can get used to it, but they never learn to read with their right brain.

Para 7: The Levy study shows us that although the left brain is specialised for language it is not very good a facial recognition, which is dealt with much more effectively by the right brain. This finding ties in well with our understanding of the importance of the right brain in disorders such as prosopagnosia. From other research we know that humans are very good at recognising faces, and Levy's study proves that this is a right-brain skill.

Para 8: Generally, split brain research is not done much these days and it is important to remember that the work that has been done has involved people who have incurred brain damage due to severe epilepsy. Thus the conclusions that we draw must take these factors into account. However, there can be little doubt that the research generally has added substantially to psychologists' understanding of the localisation of function debate, and helped to establish the role of the corpus callosum in the development of it.

General comments on practice essay 1

The two halves of the question require a clear understanding of the split brain procedure and the experimental investigation of it. Q1a asks for a description of some experimental work, and Q1b requires assessment of it in the context of localisation of function. The answers provided are not without merit, but they are partial, and display some ignorance both of the actual experimental procedures used and the interpretation that we can put on the findings. This answer might be given a mark of about 12/24 (grade C). The first part would get about 5/12 because it is limited, and lacking in detail. The second part may get a mark of around 7/12 because there is a reasonable effort to answer the question, and the material presented has been quite effectively used.

In Q1a, the choice of studies to be described is sensible, but the actual descriptions themselves are incomplete and include several errors or misunderstandings. It is, for example, apparent that the candidate has little or no idea of the way that visual information is relayed from the eye to the brain. (The important point is not which eye the information is presented to but which visual field.) Had the connections between visual field and left–right hemisphere been spelled out to start with (perhaps instead of the correct but unnecessary preamble in para 1), a much less confusing picture might then have been painted of Gazzaniga and Sperry's classic study.

It would also have helped if the candidate had said why stimuli needed to be presented via a tachistoscope. The fact that the candidate did not explain this suggests that they didn't know, or were unaware of the importance of brief presentations ... namely to avoid eye movements, and ensure that visual images only go to one or other hemisphere.

In Q1b, there is a fair attempt to relate the experimental findings to the wider issue of localisation of function, but the meaning of this is never properly spelled out, and there is a blurring of boundaries between it and the related but distinct issue of lateralisation. Whilst one could use Gazzaniga's study to reinforce the view that most language skills are mediated by the left hemisphere, a good answer might mention that some rudimentary language skills were observed in the right hemispheres of split brain subjects.

Levy's study is, effectively, misreported, and therefore difficult to link to the broader literature. In fact, Levy's study does not show that the left hemisphere cannot identify faces (it can). Rather, that in a *recognition* paradigm the input that went to the right hemisphere 'wins the day', as it were, because the subject generally chooses the face that projected to the right hemisphere (rather than the one that projected to the left) in a recognition test.

The closing paragraph rightly draws attention to the 'atypical' nature of subjects in split brain studies, but nevertheless then makes rather too much of the importance of this area of research in the context of the localisation of function debate generally.

The essay could easily have been improved if the candidate had given more thought to the difference between localisation of function and lateralisation, and especially if the descriptions of the experimental investigations had been more thorough and contained fewer errors. It is always a good idea to conclude an essay such as this with a warning about the limitations of the procedures or methods used. Although the candidate attempts this, there are other shortcomings of the split brain procedure that should be mentioned.

Specific comments

Para 1: Split brain surgery has never been 'common', and it was never intended as a cure for epilepsy; only to restrict seizures to one hemisphere. Scientists knew the real function of the corpus callosum by this time, this is why they lesioned it! Nevertheless, a good choice of exemplar studies.

Para 2: Stimuli were presented to either the right or left visual fields, not eyes. The pencil would have to be projected to the right visual field in order for the subject to say what it was.

Para 3: This depends on which visual field the image was originally projected to. An image projected to the left visual field (right hemisphere) could be drawn with the left hand for example.

Para 4: The report of Levy's study is too brief. The point needs to be made that the faces were composed in such a way that the left side face would be projected to the right hemisphere and vice versa for the right side face. The similarity (or otherwise) of the two sides of the chimeric image is irrelevant.

Para 5: Skills rather than tasks are thought to be localised. The reported studies actually say nothing about the localisation of spatial skills, although other studies have addressed this issue.

Para 6: The observation is actually a negative one, in that it suggests that the right hemisphere (not brain) does not deal with language; although other findings do support this claim. The writer reports one such finding, but once again confuses eye with visual field. The split brain studies did find evidence of rudimentary language skills in the right hemisphere.

Para 7: Levy's findings are misrepresented. The left hemisphere could identify faces, but usually reported the half face that was projected to the right visual field. A valid attempt to relate this to prosopagnosia nevertheless.

Para 8: Sensible warnings about reading too much into split brain research, which the writer then ignores! This line of research says very little about the role of the corpus callosum in the development of localisation (callosal agenesis is more relevant for this point).

Practice essay 2

(a) **Describe two or more methods or techniques used to investigate cortical functioning. (12 marks)**

(b) **Assess the strengths and weaknesses of these methods and techniques. (12 marks)** **[AEB Summer 1997]**

Candidate's answer to (a)

Para 1: There are three main approaches to measuring cortical functioning. Lesion and ablation techniques involve cutting-out certain regions of brain and then seeing what effects this has on the person. However, because of the ethical implications of these procedures, they are not used much these days, although it is possible to 'freeze' the brain temporarily. This procedure is done by giving a drug which causes a rapid drop in temperature, preventing that part of the brain from working properly for about half an hour.

Para 2: Electrical recordings have provided valuable information about the structure and function of the brain. The EEG (electrical evaluation graph) has been extensively used to record brain waves in sleep research. Small electrodes are implanted into the subject's brain and recordings are taken whilst the subject lies quietly in the recording room asleep. The EEG can indicate whether or not the subject is experiencing dreams, or having an epileptic seizure. Another form of EEG known as ERP (event related potentials) can be used on people who are awake. It involves the measurement of electrical responses in the brain following a series of events. The ERP can indicate whether or not the subject is suffering from mental illness or has been taking drugs.

Para 3: Recently, in-vivo imaging techniques have become much more popular replacing the procedures I have mentioned above for the measurement of brain function. Three in-vivo techniques deserve particular attention: CAT, MRI and PET. CAT scans provide images of the brain (rather like X-rays). This technique can be used to examine the regions of brain involved in different sorts of psychological function such as memory, learning or attention. MRI scans are even better than CAT but effectively do the same job. The main difference is that MRI does not involve as much radioactivity.

Para 4: The best in-vivo technique is, however, PET (positive emission tomography). This technique requires the subject to swallow a small amount of radioactive sugar. This gets dissolved in the blood, and it travels to the brain. The most active cells in the brain use the most sugar so these cells become the most radioactive. A scanner that looks a little like a hairdryer can detect this. The output from the scanner gives superb quality images of the brain to allow researchers to see exactly how active different regions are.

Para 5: This technique is especially useful if it is combined with a neuropsychological test. In this way researchers can give a neuropsychological test that, for example measures attention, and then use the PET scan to see which parts of the brain are most active following the task.

Para 6: Finally PET has been used extensively in research into psychiatric disorders to discover which parts of the brain are under or overactive in different disorders. People with schizophrenia seem to have overactive brains when they hallucinate for example.

Candidate's answer to (b)

Para 7: Each of the methods I have described has some advantages and some disadvantages: lesion and ablation are rather drastic procedures which should be avoided unless all other alternatives have been exhausted, because they can cause damage. One example is the split brain surgery to cure epilepsy. Although it was quite effective, it also tended to cause irreversible brain damage in some cases. A further problem is that when you damage or remove certain regions of a person's brain, other brain regions can take on the jobs of the damaged region, which makes interpretation of the results very difficult.

Para 8: Electrical procedures like EEG and ERP are very helpful in hospitals, and provide excellent measures of cortical functioning, especially where this is suspected of being abnormal. The main problem with these methods is that they are not very helpful for finding structural abnormalities in the cortex.

Para 9: The in-vivo imaging procedures have rendered many of the earlier techniques completely redundant. These techniques allow you to see the 'living' brain … you don't have to wait until the person has died to establish evidence of damage or disease. Unfortunately, a major problem is that the subject must be exposed to radioactivity for each of these techniques. This is not only hazardous; but it can lead to further complications too.

Para 10: In CAT scans, you get superb images of the brain, and can see which parts are most active too. In PET you get colour photos of the brain, and in MRI you have 3D images. An added advantage of MRI is that exposure to radioactivity is much lower than in the other techniques. MEG is a new procedure which gives colour images of the brain as stimuli are presented to the subject. This technique is proving very popular with psychologists, who are constantly on the lookout for new measures of cortical functioning.

General comments on practice essay 2

This question asks for some description and some assessment. It also leaves open the question of how many techniques to describe. The candidate must therefore choose between 'the depth' route (writing in detail about just two techniques), or the 'breadth route' (writing in less detail about lots of techniques). In questions of this sort, the key to success is getting the balance between depth and breadth right.

Having decided which techniques to introduce the next point is to organise the material as effectively as possible. The candidate chooses three areas: lesion/ablation, electrical recording, and in-vivo imaging. For an essay of this length, the choice of procedures is a good one. However, it is apparent that his or her knowledge of these techniques is variable, and in some cases limited. (It may have been wiser for the candidate to stick with material that they know well, even if this meant sacrificing some of the breadth of the essay.)

At first reading, the student conveys the impression of knowing quite a lot about investigative techniques into brain function. However, it would have been helpful at the outset to say that there are, in fact, dozens of procedures (not three as the candidate suggests), but for the sake of clarity and brevity only a sample will be described. This sort of comment gives a good impression: it suggests that the candidate knows more than she or he is actually going to cover. The examiner cannot give credit for material that is omitted, but on the other hand, these comments are an indication of good organisation, or mastery of the relevant material.

Overall, this answer may earn a mark of about 14 or 15/24. Part (a) might receive a mark of about 7/12: it is reasonably detailed, quite effectively constructed, but limited. It also (unnecessarily) includes some evaluation, although this can be included notionally by the examiner in assessing part (b). On balance, this section also merits a mark of around 7 or even 8/12. There are errors in this part of the answer, but the material is fairly evaluated on the whole, and the answer strikes a good balance between depth and breadth. This makes for a likely overall B grade.

One matter that has been ignored throughout is the distinction between function and structure. This may appear to be a subtle point, but the question specifically asks for descriptions and comments on measures of cortical *functioning*. (MOTTO: READ THE QUESTION CAREFULLY!) The fact that the writer never addresses the distinction raises the question as to whether or not s/he understands the difference. (The structure of the answers to Q2a and b suggests not). This matter could have been mentioned at the beginning of Q2a, with a comment to the effect that some measures such as EEG relate to cortical functioning, whereas other techniques such as MRI only measure structure. A particularly good way of illustrating this distinction would have been to distinguish between CT (structure) and PET (function) at the outset. This problem also permeates the answer to Q2b as we shall see.

The other major problem with Q2a is that the material which is presented is incomplete, and contains lots of minor errors (which I identify below).

The structure of the answer to Q2b should probably follow that of the answer to Q2a (which is why initial organisation was so important). Clearly, the range of procedures available suggests that each one has specific advantages and disadvantages. However, the question requires these to be assessed in addition to being described.

There are several ways of dealing with this sort of answer but one of the most effective is to present the material in a highly structured or organised way. Clearly, the examinee needs to start his/her answer to Q2b with a brief introductory paragraph. However, thereafter, the answer might then make extensive use of headings, sub-headings, underlinings and so on. For each of the techniques mentioned in the answer to Q2a, we might have the technique underlined; then a sentence or two on strengths, weaknesses and evaluation. For example:

PET:
- Strengths: very effective in-vivo technique to produce colour coded images of the amount of activity in different brain regions
- Weaknesses: definition of image is poor, and the technique does not permit assessment of structure at all
- Evaluation: has been a very effective clinical and research technique, and is especially effective when used in combination with neuropsychological or other tests: e.g. Raichle *et al.*

All that needs to be added in conclusion is some sort of over-arching evaluative comment to the effect that the newer in-vivo techniques have been adopted enthusiastically by clinicians and researchers as an aid to better understanding brain-behaviour relationships. Perhaps a good point to finish on would be to mention the recent development of fMRI as a technique which appears to avoid most of the pitfalls of the earlier in-vivo procedures, whilst retaining many of the advantages.

If you do decide to answer a question in this way, you must remember that you are meant to be writing an essay, not a list! List-type answers certainly have their place, but the trick is to embed the highly structured part of your answer in an opening and closing paragraph or two. As I said earlier, there are several ways of tackling a question such as this, but where lots of factual material has to be covered, this is an economic and effective way of handling it.

Specific comments

Para 1: Should have started with a comment about the wide range of techniques that are now available (certainly more than three). Lesion and ablation are only ever used on humans in conjunction with necessary brain surgery. It was a good point to mention the 'freezing' technique, but the description is based largely on a vivid imagination! 'Freezing' in this context is not literal: temporary inactivity is induced by administration of a short-acting drug. This is the principle of the Wada test for example. More could have been said about the use of this procedure and it could have been named.

Para 2: EEG is the abbreviation for electroencephalogram. It is usually recorded with 'surface' rather than 'implanted' electrodes. ERP is not at all well explained: the key point is that by averaging many snippets of EEG for brief periods following stimulus presentation you average away the random background EEG, and leave the ERP waveform intact. The candidate does not appear to understand the importance of the timing of this procedure. The examples of the use of EEG and ERP are helpful but could be made more clear. EEG has been used extensively in sleep research, but can actually measure brain activity in waking subjects just as well. Perhaps just one good example would be better than several partial ones. EEG and ERP are not helpful in identifying structural abnormalities.

Para 3: In-vivo techniques have quickly become assimilated, but they have not entirely replaced other procedures. CT/CAT scans are a little like composite X-rays but they measure structure, not function. They are thus of no use in researching psychological functions like memory or attention. Similarly, MRI is not a functional measure, although fMRI certainly is, and this should have been mentioned.

Para 4: PET stands for positron (not positive) emission tomography. The radioactive marker is injected or inhaled, not swallowed. The scanner is circular, but does not resemble a hair dryer (this is a confusion with MEG). PET images of the brain are very unclear, and structural abnormalities cannot usually be identified with this technique. Otherwise quite a helpful paragraph, although most researchers would judge fMRI the 'best' in-vivo technique because it combines functional and structural imaging.

Para 5: Useful comment, but the example is not a good one, and also suggests a misunderstanding of the procedure. The point is to record PET at the same time that the subject completes a neuropsychological test (not after it). Raichle's or Silbersweig's work could have been introduced here to illustrate the point.

Para 6: The use of PET in psychiatry has been quite restricted until recently, although the example given is an exciting development. Unfortunately, the findings are not correctly reported. (See what Silbersweig's group actually found, which I report in Chapter 3.)

Para 7: Split brain surgery was never intended to cure epilepsy, just to control it. The very nature of this technique, and of lesion/ablation, is to induce brain damage! The last point is a good one, but needs developing. (An example of cortical 'plasticity' would strengthen this point for example.) An additional concern that might have been mentioned is that loss of function after localised damage does not necessarily mean that that particular region was the 'brain centre' for that function. It may just be part of a distributed network, which involves several other areas as well. (Early ideas about language would be a good illustration of jumping to hasty conclusions.)

Para 8: This paragraph is fine, but an example would be helpful. EEG and ERP have been used extensively beyond the hospital setting though. (The final sentence is irrelevant in the context of this question.)

Para 9: Not all in-vivo techniques involve exposure to radiation. MRI doesn't for example. Even for those that do, there is actually no evidence that they cause further complications.

Para 10: Strictly speaking CT (a structural measure) is not relevant to this answer unless the candidate goes on to make the point that it may be possible to link faulty structure with some behavioural dysfunction. PET produces colour images rather than photos. MRI does not involve radiation at all. MEG is worth a mention, but since it is a development of EEG, it should probably have appeared earlier (in para 2). fMRI should have been introduced at some stage too.

Final points

Do   plan your answer
organise the material in a natural progression
write a thoughtful summary tying up all the loose ends
make sure you have answered the question

Don't   go off at a tangent
substitute personal opinion for research evidence
include irrelevant material
spend too long on any one answer

GOOD LUCK IN YOUR EXAMINATIONS!

Glossary

The first occurrence of each of these terms is highlighted in **bold** type in the main text.

ablation the surgical removal of brain tissue.

achromatopsia loss of colour vision in either the left, right or both visual fields.

action potential an alternative name for the nerve impulse. The basic unit of information in the nervous system.

afferent or sensory neurons neurons that carry nerve impulses towards the CNS from peripheral receptors, conveying 'sense' information.

agnosias a group of neurological disorders in which there is some deficit in a perceptual skill.

alexia loss of the ability to read.

Alzheimer's disease a dementia involving progressive loss of psychological functions as a result of widespread loss of cortical and sub-cortical neurons.

amacrine cells neurons found in the retina which contribute to the formation of receptive fields.

aphasia deficit in some aspect of language comprehension or expression.

apperceptive agnosia a failure of object recognition related to posterior right-sided cortical damage.

arcuate fasciculus the principal pathway linking Wernicke's and Broca's areas.

associative agnosia a disorder of object recognition in which the individual is unable to link the perception of an object with stored information about its meaning.

astereognosis an agnosic condition in which objects cannot be recognised by touch.

asymmetry of function another term for lateralisation, or the division of labour between the cortical hemispheres.

autonomic nervous system (ANS) part of the peripheral nervous system which controls involuntary muscles linked to internal organs such as the heart and gut.

biopsy the removal of tissue (in a living individual) for analysis.

bi-polar cell a type of neuron in the retina which acts as the bridge between photoreceptors (rods and cones) and retinal ganglion cells.

blindsight a disorder in which although unable to 'see' objects or light, individuals still seem able to avoid bumping into objects, and able to turn their heads towards objects.

blob a core region in a V1 module which contains neurons sensitive to colour.

bottom-up *See* **top-down**.

brain death the absence of detectable electrical activity in cells in the brain stem (used as an index of death).

callosal agenesis malformation or absence of the corpus callosum.

complex cells a type of visual cortical cell sensitive to moving bars of light.

conduction aphasia an aphasic condition in which the principle deficit is the inability to repeat spoken language.

cones photoreceptors in the retina sensitive to colour.

contralateral control the arrangement whereby one side of the brain receives input from, and sends output to, the opposite side of the body.

corpus callosum the main pathway linking the two hemispheres, comprising in humans about 200,000,000 myelinated neurons.

cortex the outer surface of the brain, having, in the higher mammals, a bumpy creased appearance.

cortical blindness a form of visual impairment resulting from damage to the visual cortex. As distinct from blindness linked to damage to the eyes, or visual pathways.

distributed control the neuropsychological theory that argues that most psychological functions are determined/controlled by the action of a series of interconnected brain regions

divergence the principle that, because axons branch, a single neuron can influence many target sites.

dorsal columns a set of ascending pathways towards the back of the spinal cord which carry 'fine-grained' sensory input in the somatosensory system.

double dissociation an important phenomenon in neuropsychology that helps to establish the behavioural functions of different brain regions. For example, if damage to region A affects behaviour 1 but not 2, and damage to region B affects behaviour 2 but not 1, it is probable that behaviour 1 depends on region A, and that behaviour 2 depends on region B.

efferent or motor neurons myelinated neurons carrying nerve impulses from the spinal cord to muscles.

fluent aphasia another name for Wernicke's aphasia. Language is 'fluent' but nonsensical.

ganglia clusters of cell bodies of neurons (singular: ganglion).

glial cells The name for non-neuronal cells which play a variety of supportive roles in the nervous system, and outnumber neurons 10:1. Also known as glia or neuroglia.

global aphasia a widespread failure in both receptive and expressive language function.

grandmother cells the tongue-in-cheek name for neurons towards the front of the WHAT stream linked to recognition of very specific stimuli (such as one's grandmother).

grey matter the name given to unmyelinated axons in the CNS or more commonly brain cell bodies. They are actually pinky-grey in appearance.

gyrus a elongated bump (convexity) in the cortex.

hallucinations perceptual experiences unrelated to physical sensation. They may occur in any sensory modality, and are often associated with mental illness.

hard-wired the theory that the connections in the nervous system, once determined, cannot change.

hemiplegia loss of sensory awareness from and muscle control of one side of the body.

Heschl's gyrus another name for the primary auditory cortex in the superior (top) temporal lobe.

horizontal cells a type of neuron which (like amacrine cells) contributes to the formation of receptive fields in the retina.

Huntington's chorea a rare genetically determined neurological disorder causing dementia and death due to progressive loss of neurons in the basal ganglia.

hypercomplex cells a type of visual cortical cell described by Hubel and Weisel as being particularly sensitive to moving corners or ends of objects.

inter-blob region the neurons within a module that enclose or circle the central blob region. These neurons tend to respond to stimulus features other than colour.

interneurons the name for neurons that receive input from neurons and send their output to other neurons, found throughout the CNS.

lateralisation another term for asymmetry of function, or division of labour between the hemispheres.

lesion a cut (or severing) of brain tissue. This may occur as a result of an accident, or be done as a surgical procedure.

module the basic units of visual information processing in V1: each module receives visual input from a tiny region of the retina, and deals with initial registration of colour, stimulus orientation, contrast and some movement.

myelin sheath the wrapping around the axons of many neurons giving a characteristic white appearance and leading to faster nerve impulse propagation.

nerve net a primitive unstructured nervous system found in certain aquatic creatures, made up of neurons which link to one another in an apparently haphazard way.

nerves the technical name for a bundle of axons running alongside one another.

neurons the cell type that conveys nerve impulses around the nervous system and interacts synaptically with other neurons or muscles.

nucleus (pl. nuclei) (like ganglia) the name for a bundle of neuron cell bodies in the CNS.

open head injury a head injury involving damage to the cranium, so that the brain is 'exposed' (visible). Often compared with a 'closed head' injury in which brain damage has occurred although the cranium has not been penetrated, e.g. brain damage associated with boxing.

Parkinson's disease a neurological disorder in which movements become slowed. Rigidity and tremor are also found. Associated with loss of cells in and around the basal ganglia.

percept the 'whole' that is perceived by putting together the constituent parts.

peripheral nervous system in mammals, all neuronal tissue outside the brain and spinal cord.

pigmented epithelium the layer of tissue at the back of the retina that light is reflected off in order to stimulate the rods and cones.

plastic in neuropsychology, the idea that the nervous system is not hard-wired, and that, under certain circumstances, it can alter its connections.

post-mortem a physical examination after death. In neuropsychology; usually of the brain or some other part of the nervous system.

pre-frontal area the most anterior (forward) regions of the frontal lobes. Damage to this area can impair judgement and planning, and affect personality.

pre-motor cortex the region of frontal lobe between the primary motor area and the pre-frontal area. Damage here affects the co-ordination of movements; especially those prompted by external stimuli.

primary motor cortex the region of the frontal lobes containing neurons that directly affect the movement of muscles (the rear-most gyrus).

primary sensory cortex the region(s) of cortex that deal with initial registration of sensory input, such as the somatosensory strip for touch, or V1 for visual input.

prosodic an adjective to describe emotionally intoned language. (Aprosodic speech is devoid of emotional intonation, or mono-tone.)

prosopagnosia an agnosic condition in which the individual has great difficulty in recognising faces.

psycholinguistics the psychological study of the structure and use of language.

pure word deafness a linguistic disorder in which the individual can hear words, but cannot associate meaning to them.

retinal ganglion cells the main 'output' neurons from the retina, carrying nerve impulses from the eye into the brain. The axons of these cells form the optic nerve.

rods the most numerous photoreceptors in the eye, sensitive to light but not colour.

simple cells in Hubel and Weisel's model, the type of V1 cell sensitive to stimulus orientation.

skeletal nervous system an old term for the peripheral nervous system excluding the autonomic components.

spino-thalamic tract one of two major afferent pathways in the somatosensory system conveying sensory information up the spinal cord to the brain.

stroke a catch-all term for disturbances in the blood supply to the brain. Most commonly, they are caused by obstruction to, or rupture of, blood vessels in the brain.

sulcus a small fold or crease in the cortex. Larger ones are called fissures.

supplementary motor area or SMA a region of the frontal lobe just in front of the primary motor strip involved in the co-ordination of movements; especially those that are internally planned.

synaptic transmission the chemically (or occasionally electrically) mediated communication between one neuron and another, or between a neuron and muscle.

top-down/bottom-up in psychology, the idea that there are different approaches to studying an issue. Sometimes it helps to start with a general idea, and then explore this in more detail (top-down approach). On other occasions, it may be necessary to start with specific examples, and then fit these into a broader context (bottom-up approach).

topographically represented the mapping of external space or regions of body surface in the respective primary sensory cortex. Topographic representation is particularly clearly defined in the visual and somatosensory modalities.

tracts like nerves, tracts comprise sets of axons running side by side from one part of the CNS to another.

trans-cortical aphasia a type of aphasia in which individuals can repeat and understand words, but cannot speak spontaneously.

transduction in neurophysiology, the process of converting an external energy form into action potentials, to signal stimulus presence and intensity.

trichromatic pertaining to colour vision, the trichromatic theory argues that colour vision depends on the selective sensitivity of three distinct populations of cone sensitive to red, green and blue stimuli.

ventricles the fluid filled cavities in the brain. Mammals have four, accounting for 20% to 25% of the space in the cranium.

Wada test a test which involves the administration of a fast acting barbiturate (via the carotid artery) to one hemisphere at a time to determine, amongst other things, the hemisphere which is dominant for language.

Wechsler Adult Intelligence Scales (the WAIS) A battery of verbal and non-verbal tests used to provide a comprehensive assessment of intelligence.

white matter the term used to identify myelinated nerve tissue (axons) found throughout the nervous system but particularly in the brain and spinal cord.

working memory an alternative name for short-term memory.

References

Annett, M. (1985) *Left, Right, Hand and Brain*, London: Erlbaum.

Banich, M.T. (1997) *Neuropsychology: The Neural Bases of Mental Function*, Houghton Mifflin.

Bartholomeus, B. (1974) Effects of task requirements on ear superiority for sung speech, *Cortex* 10, 215–23.

Benowitz, L. I., Finkelstein, S., Levine, D. N. and Moya, K. (1990) The role of the right cerebral hemisphere in evaluating configurations, in C. Trevarthen (ed.) *Brain Circuits and Functions of the Mind*, Cambridge University Press.

Best, C.T., Hoffman, H. and Glanville, B.B. (1982) Development of infant ear asymmetries for speech and music, *Perception and Psychophysics* 31, 75–85.

Broca, P. (1861) Remarques sur la siège de la faculté du langage articulé, *Bulletin de la Société Anatomique de Paris* 16, 343–57.

Corsi, P.M. (1972) Human memory and the medial temporal region of the brain, Ph.D. dissertation, Montreal: McGill University.

Damasio, H. and Damasio, A.R. (1989) *Lesion Analysis in Neuropsychology*, New York: Oxford University Press.

Dejerine, J. (1892) Contribution à l'étude anatomo-pathologique et clinique des différentes variétés de cécité verbale, *Comptes Rendus des Séances de la Société de Biologie et de ses Filiales* 4, 61–90.

Delis, D.C., Robertson, L.C. and Efron, R. (1986) Hemispheric specialisation of memory for visual hierarchical stimuli, *Neuropsychologia* 24 (2), 205–16.

Dennis, M. and Kohn, B. (1975) Comprehension of syntax in infantile hemiplegics after cerebral hemidecortication: Left hemisphere superiority, *Brain and Language* 2, 472–82.

Deutsch, G., Bourbon, W., Papanicolaou, A. and Eisenberg, H. (1988) Visuospatial tasks compared during activation of regional cerebral blood flow, *Neuropsychologia* 26, 445–52.

Dronkers, N. (1996) A new brain region for coordinating speech articulation, *Nature* 384, 159–61.

Farah, M.J. (1990) *Visual Agnosia: Disorders of Object Recognition and What They Tell us about Normal Vision*, Cambridge, MA: MIT Press.

Fritsch, G. and Hitzig, E. (1870) On the electrical excitability of the cerebrum, in G. von Bonin (ed.), *The Cerebral Cortex*, (1960), Springfield, IL: C.C. Thomas.

Gazzaniga, M.S. and Hillyard, S.A. (1971) Language and spatial capacity of the right hemisphere, *Neuropsychologia*, 9, 273–80.

Geffen, G. and Butterworth, P. (1992) Born with a split brain: The 15 year development of a case of congenital absence of the corpus callosum, in S. Schwartz (ed.), *Case Studies in Abnormal Psychology*, New York: John Wiley.

Geschwind, N. (1967) The varieties of naming errors, *Cortex* 3, 97–112.

Golgi, C. (1875) *Opera Omnia*, vols 1 and 2, Milan: Hoepli.

Hardyck, C. and Petrinovich, L.F. (1977) 'Left-handedness', *Psychological Bulletin* 84, 383–404.

Helmholtz, H.L.F. von. (1852) *Über die Theorie des Zusammengesetzten*, Berlin: Farben.

Hering, E. (1965) *Outlines of a Theory of the Light Sense*, trans. L.M. Hurvich and D. Jameson, Cambridge, MA: Harvard University Press.

Hubel, D. and Weisel, T. (1968) Receptive fields and functional architecture of monkey striate cortex, *Journal of Physiology* 195, 215–43.

Kalat, J.W. (1995) *Biological Psychology*, 5th edn, Brookes/Cole.

Kimura, D. (1992) Sex differences in the brain, *Scientific American* 267 (3), 118–25.

Kimura, D. and Hampson, E. (1994) Cognitive pattern in men and women is influenced by fluctuations in sex hormones, *Current Directions in Psychological Science* 3, 57–61.

Kolb, B. and Whishaw, I.Q. (1996) *Fundamentals of Human Neuropsychology*, 4th edn, New York: Freeman & Co.

Levy, J. (1969) Possible basis for the evolution of lateral specialisation of the human brain, *Nature* 224, 614–15.

Levy, J., Trevarthen, C.W. and Sperry, R.W. (1972) Perception of bilateral chimeric figures following 'hemispheric deconnection', *Brain* 95, 61–78.

Lichtheim, L. (1885) On aphasia, *Brain* 7, 433–84.

Lissauer, H. (1890) Ein Fall von Seelenblindheit nebst einem Beitrage zur Theorie derselben, *Archiv fur Psychiatrie und Nervenkrankheiten* 21, 222–70.

Livingstone, M. and Hubel, D. (1988) Segregation of form, colour, movement and depth: anatomy, physiology and perception, *Science* 240, 740–9.

Loewi, O. (1960) An autobiographical sketch. *Perspectives in Biological Medicine* 4, 3–25.

Luria, A.R. (1966) *Higher Cortical Functions in Man*, New York: Basic Books.

MacCoby, E. and Jacklin, C. (1974) *The Psychology of Sex Differences*, Stanford, CA: Stanford University Press.

McGlone, J. (1980) Sex differences in human brain asymmetry: A critical survey, *Behavioural and Brain Sciences* 3 (2), 215–63.

McNeil, J.E. and Warrington, E.K. (1993) Prosopagnosia: A face specific disorder, *Quarterly Journal of Experimental Psychology* 46 (a), 1–10.

Mersenich, M.M. and Kaas, J.H. (19800) Principles of organisation of sensory-perceptual systems in mammals, in J.M. Sprague and A.N. Epstein (eds), *Progress in Psychobiology and Physiological Psychology*, vol. 9, New York: Academic Press.

Milner, B. (1963) Effects of different brain lesions on card sorting, *Archives of Neurology* 9, 90–100.

—— (1971) Inter-hemispheric differences in the location of psychological processes in man, *British Medical Journal* 27, 272–7.

Mogilner, A., Grossman, J.A., Ribary, U., Joliot, M., Volkman, J., Rapaport, D., Beasley, R.W. and Llinas, R.R. (1993) Somatosensory cortical plasticity in adult humans revealed by magnetoencephalography, *Proceedings of the National Academy of Sciences* 90, 3593–7

Money, J.A. (1976) *A Standardised Road Map Test of Directional Sense. Manual*, San Rafael, CA: Academic Therapy Publications.

Naeser, M.A. and Hayward, R.W. (1978) Lesion localisation in aphasia with cranial computed tomography and the Boston Diagnostic Aphasia Exam, *Neurology* 28, 545–51.

Nieuwenhuys, R., Voodg, J. and van Huijzen, C. (1988) *The Human Central Nervous System: A Synopsis and Atlas*, Berlin: Springer-Verlag.

Penfield, W., and Boldrey, E. (1958) Somatic motor and sensory representation in the cerebral cortex as studied by electrical stimulation, *Brain* 60, 389–443.

Petersen, S.E. and Fiez, J.A. (1993) The processing of single words studied with positron emission tomography, *Annual Review of Neuroscience* 16, 509–30.

Raichle, M.E. (1994) Visualising the mind, *Scientific American* 269 (1), 36–42.

Ramon y Cajal, S. (1989) *Recollections of My Life*, Cambridge, MA: MIT Press.

Reitan, R.M. and Wolfson, D. (1993) *The Halstead-Reitan Neuropsychological Test Battery: Theory and Clinical Interpretation*, Tucson, AZ: Neuropsychology Press.

Roland, P.E. (1993) *Brain Activation*, New York: Wiley-Liss.

Rosenzweig, M.R., Leiman, A.L. and Breedlove, S.M. (1996) *Biological Psychology*, Sunderland, MA: Sinauer Associates Inc, p.60.

Sacks, O. (1985) *The Man Who Mistook his Wife for a Hat*, New York: Summit Books.

Semmes, J., Weinstein, S., Ghent, L. and Teuber, H.L. (1955) Spatial orientation: Analysis of locus of lesion, *Journal of Psychology* 39, 227–44.

Sergent, J. (1982) The cerebral balance of power: Confrontation or cooperation?, *Journal of Experimental Psychology (Human Perception and Performance)* 8, 252–272.

—— (1990) Further incursions into bicameral minds, *Brain* 113, 537–68.

Sergent, J. and Signoret, J.L. (1992) Functional and anatomical decomposition of face processing: Evidence from prosopagnosia and PET study of normal individuals, *Philosophical Transactions of the Royal Society of London* B335, 55–62.

Silbersweig, D.A., Stern, E., Frith, C., Cahill, C., Holmes, A., Grootoonk, S., Seaward, J., McKenna, P., Chua, S.E., Schnorr, L., Jones, T. and Frackowiak, R.S.J. (1995) A functional neuroanatomy of hallucinations in schizophrenia, *Nature* 378, 176–9.

Smith, E.E. and Jonides, J. (1994) 'Working memory in humans: Neuropsychological evidence', in M.S. Gazzaniga (ed.), *The Cognitive Neurosciences*, pp. 1009–20, Cambridge, MA: MIT Press.

Sperry, R.W., Gazzaniga, M.S. and Bogen, J.E. (1969) 'Inter-hemispheric relationships: The neocortical commisures; syndromes of hemisphere disconnection', in P.J. Vinken and G.W. Bruyn (eds), *Handbook of Clinical Neurology*, vol. 4, pp. 273–90, New York: John Wiley & Sons.

Starr, C. and Taggart, R. (1989) *Biology: The Unity and Diversity of Life*, 5th edn, Belmont, CA: Wadsworth (now Thomson).

Stirling, J., Wilkinson, A. R. and Cavill (1999) [In press]

Taylor, L.B. (1969) Localisation of cerebral lesions by psychological testing, *Clinical Neurosurgery* 16, 269–87.

Wada, J. and Rasmussen, T. (1960) Intracarotid injection of sodium amytal for the lateralisation of cerebral speech dominance, *Journal of Neurosurgery* 17, 266–82.

Warrington, E.K. (1982) Neuropsychological studies of object recognition, *Philosophical Transactions of the Royal Society of London* B298, 15–33.

Warrington, E.K. and Taylor, A.M. (1978) Two categorical stages of object recognition, *Perception* 7, 695–705.

Wechsler, D. (1981) *Manual for the Wechsler Adult Intelligence Scale – Revised*, San Antonio, TX: Psychological Corporation.

Wernicke, C. (1874) *Der aphasische Symptomenkomplex*, Breslau: Cohn & Weigert.

Wickelgren, I. (1997) Getting a grasp on working memory, *Science* 275, 1580–2.

Young, T. (1802) The Bakerian lecture: On the theory of light and colours, *Philosophical Transactions of the Royal Society, London*, 12–48.

Zeki, S. (1992) The visual image in mind and brain, *Scientific American* 267 (3), 68–76.

Index